Remarkable You

A Journey to Discover HOPE Within

Wendy Burns

SKINNY BROWN DOG MEDIA
www.SkinnyBrownDogMedia.com

Remarkable You: A Journey to Discover HOPE Within
2nd Edition

Copyright © Wendy Burns 2022
All rights reserved.

No part of this book may be reproduced or transmitted in any form or by any means, electronic or mechanical, including photocopying, recording or by any information storage and retrieval system, without prior permission in writing from the publisher.

Published by Skinny Brown Dog Media
Atlanta, USA and Punta del Este, UY
www.skinnybrowndogmedia.com
Distributed by Skinny Brown Dog Media
Developmental Editing and Design by Eric G. Reid
Content Editing by Timothy Swiney

ebook: 978-1-957506-16-6
Hardback ISBN: 978-1-957506-17-3
Paperback ISBN: 978-1-957506-18-0

The names of some people in this book have been changed to protect their identities.

You are invited
on a journey through
HOPE
to
DISCOVER
UNSHACKLE
REVEAL
and
ENABLE
the REMARKABLE YOU within!

Commendations for

Remarkable You

"Wendy, bring me my gun…"

She handed it to him and he said, "this is how you kill yourself!"

Dad took the rifle and loaded it, placed the barrel in his mouth and pulled the trigger.

I was there when this happened. I can vividly remember us running screaming and crying down Bundarra Rd, Uralla. It was Saturday 21st May 1966, Wendy was 13 and I was four.

But this is not my story, this is Wendy's story. I have no idea how she felt and what she went through for so many years, carrying the misplaced guilt for handing our father the gun he killed himself with. That life event was just the catalyst to circumstances that dealt many harsh blows, that some people might look at and be dismayed, even horrified, at how a person copes or gets through such things.

Wendy struggled at times as we all did and still do, some didn't make it out the other side without irreparable scars. Wendy would tell you though that this was 'just her life—her story' unique to her, 'harder than some and not as hard as others' 'it all depends on your perspective'.

How she got through, and is still getting through, to become this amazing, loving, caring and beautifully flawed woman is a story of courage, resilience, hope and the Grace of God.

"He doesn't love some future version of you; He loves you in all your mess."

Steve, Wendy's little brother

Two Aussies first met all the way over in Orlando Florida USA, due to a shared mentor, John C Maxwell and a shared passion to add value to others. In these past few years, Wendy has become a partner, a collaborator and, more importantly, a friend of mine and a part of my family's future.

It is this proximity that puts me in position to tell you that Wendy is the real deal. And she gets very real with you here in this book. You may care about what she knows and you will definitely know that she cares about you, the reader—the **Remarkable You**!

If you need to borrow someone's belief in you at this point—that's okay—Wendy is the perfect choice for a 'new voice' to consider. Allow her gutsy and vivid vulnerability in this book to deal hope to you and cheer you on in your next steps to 'shake off the legacy of your circumstances.'

Jason Ewart
Author, Coach, Trainer, Mentor

Every once in a while you pick up a book, a remarkable book that reveals the compassionate heart of the author for those that society has written off.

Having known Wendy personally as a friend and having shared the stage with her professionally, I am amazed at how someone who has been through so much can turn out so good. All I can say is, it's nothing short of a miracle! The warmth, care and integrity that Wendy exudes is remarkable. Throughout all the dark and life-defining battles, she has continued to hold her head up high.

Maybe it was the outworking of a divine plan so that one day her story would inspire and help lift the heads of countless others.

This book is bound to take you on a journey. One where you feel you get to peek into someone's life and see their lives play out right before your very eyes. It's as if you have the very best seats in the theatre of her life, and when the spotlight is shone center-stage, you can't help but be drawn in by the tragedy of the soul that's laid bare before you. Somehow, someway you feel a deep connection with what you are witnessing.

Wendy's story is one of hope, courage and victory. It draws us towards a deeper longing for healing, something we all desire yet find difficult to articulate. Throughout the pages of this book, you'll draw encouragement from Wendy's remarkable journey and when the final pages are turned, you'll walk away empowered and filled with hope and possibilities. I pray that Wendy will continue to empower, encourage and inspire thousands with her wonderful message of hope and victory.

This book is a book of life lessons. When we apply what we learn here to our own lives, I believe it will truly reveal the remarkable within us. Thank you, Wendy, for entrusting us with your story. You truly are remarkable and now we know we can be too!

Christopher Sajnendra
Coach to CEOs, Life and Success Strategist, Entrepreneur, Author, Speaker, Pharmacist & Hope Dealer.

My first meeting with Wendy was when I attended her Blueprint for Success Workshop in 2015. My first & lasting impression was how warm, kind, capable & professional she was. The warmth & compassion that Wendy portrayed through her teaching & facilitation that day was comforting & inspiring.

Four years on, Wendy continues to be a beautiful presence in my life. We have developed a friendship that is based on a mutual respect of honoring & supporting one another's individual journeys.

Wendy's past is heart wrenching. But that was her past. She has shown that it is possible to survive anything. No matter what has happened to you, you can survive. If you are still breathing, you can thrive, despite the trauma; abuse & painful memories.

Writing helps you to heal, it is a cathartic process & once the words are on the page it is released from your body. Wendy's decision to share her story came from a place of personal transformation. A desire & willingness to help others who may be going through that space of darkness themselves.

Wendy knows she no longer must endure the darkness alone. She is surrounded by love. Love is like lighting a candle to diffuse the darkness. Shame, negativity & fear dissolve & hope is what remains.

My dear, brave & remarkable friend—I'll always be here to listen.

Tanya Olssen
Friend and Registered Yoga Therapist

Acknowledgments

It's important to me that I take a moment to acknowledge those who have traveled with me on this journey.

My darling husband Bill: We have journeyed together through many different landscapes in our lives. You have seen the worst and the best of me as I have journeyed to discover who I was. You stayed through the good, bad and ugly moments of our lives together and we have gone on to forge 42 years of marriage. Know my love for you grows deeper every day.

My children: Warwick, Michelle, Darren and Karen, each one of you are significant in my life and loved dearly as are every one of my grandchildren. Beau, Maddison, Lotus, Pixie, Blossom, Harrison, Riley, Savannah, Catalina, Joanne and Jack, know that because of my journey to discover hope, that the generational inheritance that you now have, sets you on a path to reach the highest and greatest possibilities to live to the very best of the **remarkable** within each of you. I love you and believe in each one of you.

To my brother Steve: Thank you for encouraging me to tell my story, your prayers, your love and your support. *Steven, yours is a story that needs to be told.*

My beautiful sister Gail: I am proud of you for staying the journey and finding your way. You have each been on your own journeys and the challenges along that journey. Each of you has faced in your own way, the challenges thrown at you from birth, but each of you have not given in and come through the other side. Very proud of you both, love you dearly. *Continue to journey well!*

To my beautiful sisters Carol and Shirley Kerri: Our lives are a never-ending story in which we are scripted, made up of many different chapters. Your chapters of life have sadly been cut way too short. They began with the delight you gave Mum and Dad and Gail, Steven and me. So much joy, in a life that had little and you became the delight of our lives. You left the imprint of your love on our lives. Your challenges were BIG and with each one I watched you. You both took on and tried to overcome these challenges until you could no longer fight the battles. The chapters of your life have closed, but new chapters begin where your legacy is carried, and shines bright by your beautiful children and grandchildren, brother and sisters. You will always be missed greatly and always in our hearts. I know you wait for us in Heaven. Rest well.

To my sisters-in-law who have become just like my own flesh and blood: You may never have known the challenge it was for me to join such an amazing family. Thank you for staying the journey with me, even when I was not so nice to be around. You are much loved and appreciated, Alice-Anne, Susie and Kathryn (Kassy).

To my sister-in-law Karen: thank you for your unconditional love.

To those of you that became my cheer-squad: friends, mentors, teachers as mentioned in my story, my bosses in government, the many that believed in me, prayed for me and stood by me, even when I did not believe in myself. You may never know the importance of your impact on my life and the significance of the belief you placed in me. Know that it was not wasted. I value each and every one of you. Thank you.

To Nicholas from Nickreative for being part of my journey and capturing that with your photography and creative design. A Remarkable Man, thank you!

To Eric Reid my Editor and Publisher, Skinny Brown Dog Media: thank you for your eye for details, generous wisdom, and creativity, you are very much appreciated.

Wendy Burns

Contents

Foreword	1
Before We Set Out	3
Content Warning	7
How to Use this Book	11
Chapter 1: Inheriting Hopelessness from Your Circumstances	15
Chapter 2: Believing You are Responsible	23
Chapter 3: The Fundamental Need to Belong	31
Chapter 4: Numbing the Pain	39
Chapter 5: The Downward Spiral	45
Chapter 6: A Vision of Hope	51
Chapter 7: The Bogus Stories in our Baggage	57
Chapter 8: The Seed of Hope	65
Chapter 9: Becoming a Futurist	73
Chapter 10: A Change of Attitude	79
Chapter 11: Growing Belief in Yourself	87
Chapter 12: Choosing the people around you	93
Chapter 13: The Dangers of Hidden Baggage	99
Chapter 14: Growing Self-worth	107
Chapter 15: Fighting for Your Remarkable Self	113
Chapter 16: A True Battle Moment	123
Chapter 17: Remarkable Me	133
Chapter 18: Remarkable YOU	141
Final Travel Advisory	149
Essential Items for Remarkable Travelers	151
Epilogue: My Trust in God	153
About the Author	157

Foreword

This is a story of a battle royal.

It is an extraordinary example of how a person can overcome some of the worst early experiences in one's life, and become a fully functioning contributor to their own life and the lives of others. Wendy lived through multiple toxic stressors as a young child, and these days the resulting damage would be called PTSD.

The shame she speaks of is one of the emotional harms suffered by children who should be able to trust their caregivers and extended family—it is profoundly destructive when not balanced with nurture and empathy—both of these things Wendy almost had to find for herself, and it was, finally, her relationship with a nurturing and trustworthy 'other'—her God, who provided the wings for her flight to good mental, emotional and spiritual health.

I came to know Wendy when she was working in HR for the government department she mentions. She became my 'inside' go-to person who could support the folk I was working with. This work often involved difficult and challenging conflict resolution processes, and Wendy's relational skills and sheer compassion and empathy supported staff through these processes. During that time, she soaked up this style of work and its philosophy around accountability, responsibility and healing. When it became her turn to lead and manage others in that same government department, her integrity shamed others, and so began the nonsense that almost destroyed her again.

In his extraordinary book *The Boy Who Was Raised as a Dog,* Bruce Perry sums up Wendy's journey for me:

> *The more healthy relationships a child has, the more likely he will be able to recover from trauma and thrive. Relationships are the agents of change and the most powerful therapy is human love* (2017, p. 258)

But somewhere in all that, her emerging faith in herself as a capable and competent person contributed to her hard-won resilience, and I have watched with interest and great pride as the butterfly has emerged from the chrysalis, despite multiple setbacks. What Wendy has done with her life, and how she now uses those gifts to help others who may find themselves in similar spaces in their lives, is a special story. Her life is a testament to hope, and my profound wish is that readers who are drawn to this story can find the same.

Margaret Thorsborne
Author, trainer, facilitator, fellow traveler.

Before We Set Out

"Your story matter, because YOU matter."

We all have a story, none more important than someone else's. Each story will be made up of many different chapters: some good, some bad, and some downright ugly. Mine has certainly contained all three.

No matter what our story is, we all want to feel we matter. This is a book for people struggling with that belief. I believe we all matter: I believe *you matter,* and I want to help you believe that too, whatever your circumstances are. I believe every person has within them a **Remarkable You.**

If you are reading those words and a little voice is whispering to you "she's wrong, she doesn't know how bad you are," please ignore that voice and read on, because I am here to tell you that **You Are Remarkable**.

As a child I would go looking for gold with my dad in the creeks around Uralla (New South Wales, Australia). It was very often just him and me. He told me how hard it was to find the hidden gold, and showed me how to use the panning dish to search for it.

We would take some gravel from the creek, wash it with the water and slowly slush it around, working through the grit and grime until we started to see tiny specks of gold. It was hard work to find just one speck, but he would reassure me once we found one speck of gold, we would be able to find the 'gold vein' and discover all the gold.

It is like that with people too, I have discovered. We all have gold within us, but so often it is hidden and buried beneath the rubbish we have been exposed to in life, by others and ourselves.

The **remarkable** within each one of us is the gold we are seeking. As I traveled my journey out of hopelessness, I remembered those times panning for gold with my dad, and it helped me understand changing my destiny would require hard work. I would have to slush through the muck, and grime of *bogus stories*, dark emotions and self-destructive behaviors to find the gold in me. I found the gold within me, and I know you can to.

When we are born, we do not find ourselves lacking in any way. We accept ourselves just as we are. Life and circumstances have a way of filling our heads and hearts with judgments that make all of us lose sight of the **remarkable** within, and depression and anxiety are the symptoms of the dis-ease in our lives. All of us experience our times of doubt, and insecurity.

Society often tells us that we are a result of our circumstances and that nothing can change. It tells us that we are stuck where we are and the generations that come behind us will be stuck too. This makes us feel like we are the victim of our circumstances, with no escape, no hope for change. Hopelessness is like a shackle, stopping us from stepping into our potential. We think we are not good enough, and could not possibly *do this*, or *have that.*

If you feel like you have no hope, take heart. You are not a victim of your circumstances, however difficult, however seemingly hopeless.

How do I know? I speak from personal experience.

My personal history is dark and heavy. For the first 34

years of my life, I felt like there was no hope, and no way out. Everything around me: people, circumstances and society, reinforced that thinking. I believed my life would turn out like my parents' lives, and so would my children's lives.

At 65, I am living proof that is wrong.

The heart of this book, sharing the story of my journey, is to show you how I found hope—real hope!—and how that allowed me to discover the **remarkable** within me. I have shaken off the legacy of my circumstances, and I have now used my strengths to shape a fulfilling life for myself and to help hundreds of other people do the same (find out more in About the Author, p.111).

My story will show you there *is* HOPE even where visibly there appears to be none. Hope unshackled me from my circumstances, revealed the scope of my potential and enabled the gold within me to shine: it can do it for you, too. I want you to know in the depth of your heart that your history is not your destiny. I will show you the only power our past has over us is the power we choose to give it.

You might find that hard to believe right now, but you are **remarkable**.

You are lovable.

You are worthy.

You are *remarkable*.

If you want your future to be totally unlike your past, come along with me on this journey.

Love, Wendy

Content Warning

This book makes many references to difficult, possibly triggering, topics including child abuse, drug and alcohol abuse, rape and suicide. Reading this book may bring up challenging issues for some readers. Please take care.

Help is available

If you are having suicidal thoughts, you need to stay safe and get help immediately. No matter how bad things seem, there is help for you. Please make the call.

United States

Emergency: 911
Non-emergency essential local services: 211
National Suicide Prevention Lifeline: 800-273-8255
Crisis Text Line: Text HOME TO 741741
National Alliance on Mental Illness NAMI HelpLine: 1-800-950-6264 or text NAMI to 741-741
Crisis Support Services national helpline: 800-273-8255
SAMHSA's National Helpline (substance abuse and mental health): 800-662-HELP (800-662-4357)
Teen Line for youth in need of support: 800-852-8336

Australia

Lifeline Australia—13 11 14
Beyond Blue—1300 224 636
Samaritans—135 247
Suicide Call Back Service—1300 659 467

State Crisis Numbers (Australia)

NSW—1800 011 511—Mental Health Line
VIC—1300 651 251—Suicide Help Line
QLD—13 432 584—13 HEALTH
TAS—1800 332 388—Mental Health Services Helpline
SA—13 14 65—Mental Health Assessment and Crisis Intervention Service
WA—1800 676 822—Mental Health Emergency Response Line
NT—08 8999 4988—Top End Mental Health Service
ACT—1800 629 354—Mental Health Triage Service

Canada

Talk Suicide Canada 1-833-456-4566

United Kingdom & Ireland

Samaritans National Lifeline UK & Ireland 116 123

If you or someone near you is in immediate danger, call Emergency Services or go to the nearest hospital Emergency Department.

Suicide

Suicide has a devastating impact on families, friend and whole communities. The causes of suicide are complex, but hopelessness is a common experience for people contemplating suicide. Factors that may contribute to suicide include:

- stressful life events
- trauma
- mental illness
- physical illness
- drug or alcohol abuse
- poor living circumstances.

The following facts are from The Black Dog Institute:

- Every year over 65,000 Australians make a suicide attempt.
- More than 3,000 Australians died by suicide in 2017.
- Suicide is the leading cause of death for Australians between 15 and 44 years of age.
- Young Australians are more likely to take their own life than die in motor vehicle accidents.
- In 2017, about 75% of people who died by suicide were males and 25% were females.
- In 2017, the suicide rate among Aboriginal and Torres Strait Islander people was approximately twice that of non-Indigenous Australians.

These facts can be confronting, as are elements of this book. It is tragic how many lives are lost to hopelessness, but suicide can be prevented.

How to Use this Book

This is a true story, and one that I hope will empower you to believe that you can be the author of your own story. I want my story to shine a light for you on your path. I invite you to read it with an open mind, and a willing heart.

This book can be read as a memoir: a sometimes sad and confronting story about a loved, but abused child who grew to reject the legacy of her circumstances and become a woman of influence. If that is how you read it, I hope it inspires you.

It can also be read as a self-help book. I have had the privilege of helping many people uncover the remarkable within them, so I know your story will not be the same as my story but there will be many themes in common. In each chapter, I have included focus points to enable you to reflect on my journey, and action steps to start you on your path. When you choose to take this journey of discovery, please take some time to consider the questions at the end of each chapter before moving on. You will need a notebook to use as a journal of your actions to unshackle, reveal and enable the **Remarkable You** as you read.

My sisters and brother and I experienced such terrible things as children that sometimes I find it hard to believe it was real. In the course of writing this book, I got hold of case files relating to my family. Although it was hard to read, I was forced to acknowledge what a truly difficult journey I have traveled.

As you read, know this is just an overview of some significant points. I have shared details of events I believe will enable you to see that bad chapters in our stories do not **in any way** predict a bad ending.

I refer to strong feelings, thoughts and themes throughout the chapters. I discuss how these affected me both inwardly, in my heart and mind, and how they played out in my life through my actions and behaviors on the lives of those around me. Some of this content may be difficult. Please take care.

I look forward to taking this journey with you.

Remarkable You.

Step Forward
Remarkable You

Chapter 1

Inheriting Hopelessness from Your Circumstances

I remember my father's funeral vividly. As I stood by his grave, my heart was broken. My dad was my hero. I followed him everywhere. When he was gardening, fishing, panning for gold in the creeks, working: I was there. As they lowered his coffin into that big dark hole, I fell to the ground sobbing. I was so overwhelmed with grief and guilt I could not breathe. I was the one who put him there. I had killed my dad and I was only thirteen!

At that young age, I was already nurturing the belief my life was hopeless. My parents believed it, and I inherited that belief.

I grew up in a very small country town called Uralla, in New South Wales, Australia. It was one of those towns where everyone knew everyone—and everyone's business. I was the second eldest in a family of five children. Sadly, I have lost two of my younger sisters to alcoholism.

We were a poor family. Not just money poor, but poor in every aspect and even in that little country town, we were aware of this 'poorness'. We lived in broken, run-down homes. The food we had was what my father was able to grow in his garden or catch. He used to go hunting for rabbits: setting traps and we would eat what he caught, and he would sell the skins for money. In season, both my parents would go fruit picking, because where we lived was fruit country. I can remember playing in the fruit orchards while my parents picked fruit and packed it.

Both of my parents were alcoholics, not that I knew that word then, I just knew they were just drinking all the time. As children, my three sisters: Gail, Carol and Shirley Kerri, my brother Steven and I spent a lot of time playing on the footpath outside one hotel or another, waiting while they drank. They would often end up so drunk they would have to sleep it off in the gutter.

It was part of our normal life as children, and so was the violence that is so often associated with alcoholism: violence towards us children, violence from one parent to the other. I witnessed my mother being bashed by my dad, or one of us kids being bashed, regularly—especially after a day at a hotel.

One fight in particular stands out in my memory. My father, my uncle Joe and my mother were talking as we ate lunch, on a break from picking fruit. They were talking about my dad buying a gun so he could shoot rabbits instead of trapping them. I remember my mother was angry as she did not want my dad to have a gun. It ended up in a huge fight. Perhaps my mum in some deep level knew what the consequences of his action, in buying this gun, would be. Little did I, a child, know then that this was a life changing moment for my family.

This was the pattern of our parents' lives. Working, drinking, fighting. As time passed, my eldest sister Gail and I tried to take responsibility for our sisters and brother, looking after them and feeding them as best we could, even though we were kids ourselves.

We were often dirty—cleanliness was not a priority in our home—but as a child I knew no different. This was my life, so it was my norm. As a child, until someone points out you are different, you just think that is how everyone lives. The day I realized I was different, my awareness changed. For me, as for so many of us, it happened at school.

The kids at school started to call me dirty. They told me my clothes were dirty, and I was no good. This was the first time I realized I was judged by what the world tells us our life should be, and I did not fit the picture of what the world said I should be: even in that little country town, all that time ago.

That was when I first allowed *someone else's opinion* to become *my truth*.

That was when I started to pretend, in my mind, that I lived in another family. It sounds crazy, but that is what I did. I can remember a friend asked me to stay at her house one night and I stayed for weeks. I simply did not want to go home. The reality was that my family were different: I was different. Deep inside I already believed *different* meant *bad,* and I would end up like my parents.

I did not know what shame was back then, but I have realized since that was when shame first attached itself to me.

Shame, as Dr Brené Brown has defined it in her excellent work on the topic, is the intensely painful feeling that we are so deeply flawed that we are unworthy of belonging. In other words, the belief we are such terrible humans we are not fit for human society. Hopelessness emerges from shame because when you believe you are not worthy of love, you also believe you will always stay that way, so there can never be hope of things being different. The dark feelings feed negative thoughts and beliefs which feed destructive or damaging behaviors, which in turn feed dark feelings, in a downward spiral.

With hindsight, I can see my parents had no hope. Perhaps that was the legacy they inherited from their circumstances, the belief that life could not change and get better? I am sure they felt there was no hope for their kids. Hopelessness will lead you to believe there is no way forward. That is a lie, but it took me a long time to figure that out.

One night when I was twelve, Dad took my brother, my sisters and me out into the bush in his car, a Ford Zephyr. I do not know where Mum was, but I think they had been fighting. He parked the car in the middle of nowhere and told us to get on the floor. He said he would come back to get us, and left us there. We were so very scared. I remember trying to settle the little ones down.

We were all afraid of the dark. Little did we know we had more to fear than that. Dad had run a hose from the exhaust into the window, and left the engine running. How we survived is truly a miracle: the hose fell off the exhaust.

It was only in the morning when the sun came up and

we got out of the car that we saw the results of Dad's attempt to take our lives. Gail and I gathered our sisters and brother and walked out of the bush. To this day I am not sure how we even found our way, but we did. No one except us knew what happened, because who could we tell?

It was only looking back years later that I could perceive his actions as a desperate attempt to spare us from the hopelessness he felt.

A few months later, on 21 May 1966, that world, the only life I knew, changed forever. That was the day my dad committed suicide. He was 39 years old. I was thirteen.

Reflection: Shame

It is important to take a moment to address shame. Shame is a powerful universal emotion which often emerges when we feel deeply vulnerable about something and believe that others have the power to judge us, and reject us.

It can take the form of irrational feelings of worthlessness, humiliation and self-loathing. It is a paralyzing feeling inflicted onto an individual through traumatic experiences often, but not always, rooted in childhood. We all experience it, but society tells us it is shameful to feel shame, so we suppress, or hide, or numb those dark feelings.

It is a dark, hidden secret that becomes entrenched within our hearts. Shame feeds the sense we are not okay in who we are and we could never be acceptable. Shame comes with its friends; humiliation, mortification, discredit, dishonor and disgrace, and makes us believe we are unworthy of belonging.

Shame is the ultimate *bogus story* (see chapter 7). Shame can come in when we allow other people's opinions to become our truth. Shame makes us work harder at 'fitting in' because we believe we are not good enough and cannot measure up, as we are.

If you are feeling hopeless, then you are no stranger to shame. Take the time to address the root of this shame. Identify the areas where you feel shame and how this plays out in your life: how it presents itself in your thoughts and actions. Identification is the first step to being free.

Focus Points:

- Has shame been part of your journey so far?
- Can you identify a time when you first started to feel shame about something?
- What would it feel like if you had no shame?

Action Steps for Your Journey:

- Use a journal to write down areas of your life where shame has raised its ugly head.
- Take some time over the next few days to think about how your perspective would look differently in your current circumstances and life if there was no shame. Write it in your journal.
- Take one small step to unshackle yourself from that shame, knowing that shame is the ultimate *bogus story*? When you feel ashamed, even telling yourself shame is a *bogus story* will help.

Chapter 2

Believing You are Responsible

The day my father killed himself we were supposed to go to Tamworth, another country town about 90 kilometers away, but it snowed, so my parents spent the day at the local hotel drinking instead. My brother and sisters and I waited outside, as usual.

When we got home, my parents went into separate rooms. My dad went into my room and asked me to bring him his gun, a rifle. Of course, I did: I always did what my dad asked, he was my hero. When I handed it to him, he was laying down on my bed, his head on my pillow.

He said, "This is how you kill yourself." He put the barrel of the gun in his mouth and pulled the trigger.

He blew his brains out, right there in front of me, his thirteen year old daughter.

You can only imagine what I saw.

I did not speak or scream. Shock kicked in and the horror of what I just witnessed made me grab my sisters and brother and we ran from the house. I did not want them to see what I had seen. We ran many kilometers away to a neighbors' house, a place where I felt safe, crying all the way.

In that moment I did not even think of my mother. I am not sure why. I just felt the urgency to get my siblings and take them far away from what I saw.

I was just a child, and I witnessed unthinkable things that day that were imprinted into my mind, and impacted my behavior well into my thirties. Seeing that horror changed my life in an instant, and it controlled every aspect of my life for a very long time.

The neighbors we sought help from called the police. I was interviewed about my role in my dad's death and this is where my cover-up began. That day I picked up responsibility for Dad's actions. In my 13-year-old eyes, it was very simple. I killed my dad by handing him the gun. It did not matter to me that my dad asked me to hand him his gun. It did not even enter my mind back then that there was no way I could have known what his desperate thoughts were and how they would play out.

As well as taking on the burden of guilt, that day I learned a life lesson from Dad. That day he taught me, when the pain of life gets too much, the solution is to take your own life. Another heavy burden for a child to carry.

Even though he beat me, my siblings and our mum, even though he tried to kill us, even though he blew his brains out in front of me, he was my dad, my hero. I did not want people to blame him for what happened. So I told them it was an accident. I was trying to cover up his behavior, his mistakes and I was covering for my own guilt over handing him the gun.

I remember a great sadness hung over my dad, a deep darkness in many ways. He killed the pain of life with what he put in his mouth. People do it all the time, numbing their pain with what they put in their mouths: alcohol, drugs, food, words. Dad had been diagnosed with bowel cancer and told he would have to wear a colostomy bag. I believe now the pain was too much, and his way out was to end his life. So he killed his pain by putting a gun in his mouth.

Here I go again, making excuses for him. I know we have all done it, made excuses for what our parents, our siblings, our partners, our friends have done. Giving them excuses; taking responsibility for their choices; and blaming ourselves.

The night of my dad's death, my mother, sisters and brother and I stayed with my uncle Ted (on my father's side), and his wife. I slept in the same bed with Mum to try and console her. No doubt I was in shock. I could not get the image of Dad out of my mind.

When Mum was finally sleeping, in the early hours of morning, I got up. I walked through the house crying until my uncle, who was sleeping in the room next to us said, "Come into my bed and let me comfort you." Innocently, I jumped into his bed. I had no understanding of what was about the happen. My uncle's idea of comforting me was sexual assault. Why? Simply because he could.

My aunt came into the room afterwards and told me to get out of the bed and not to tell anyone. She was angry and I was not sure if it was at me or him. I only knew that what had just happened added to my shock and horror. Once again I felt shame and my guilt mounted.

The guilt I carried from my father's suicide was overwhelming at times, and I carried that burden for far too long. The people in my life who I loved and relied on for protection exposed me to so much horror and pain in that 24 hours of my life, but it took me a long time to see how they had betrayed me. Instead, I took responsibility for things which were far beyond my control.

Dad's funeral was held in the little Catholic Church. There I was, this child with a heavy burden on her small shoulders. All I could see was the coffin and Mum next to me sobbing. As we followed the coffin out Mum clung to it, sobbing and screaming until she had to be removed. This compounded my dark feelings of guilt and shame: not only had I killed my dad but I had caused my mum so much pain she could not go on.

As the coffin was lowered into the ground, my grief and guilt overwhelmed me. What had I done? I killed my dad, my hero! Everything in our lives changed because of me! Truly it was too much for my young heart to bear. I had to be taken away.

Sadly, all too often, it is our family or friends, the people we love and are meant to protect us, who are the ones that betray us. That is their responsibility to own, not ours. We can try to cover-up for those we love and pretend it does not matter that what they are doing is not okay, and that is what I did, but truly all we can do is take responsibility for ourselves.

My 13-year-old self did not know that. I blamed myself for everything, so I made it my responsibility to fix everything. I became a control freak, but I had no understanding other people are beyond our control.

Reflection: Responsibility

"The willingness to accept responsibility for one's own life is the source from which self-respect springs."
Joan Didion

I stepped into taking responsibility for my father's actions as a 13-year-old, covering up for his choices, his decisions. I was overwhelmed, my life was out of control and my way of coping was to step up and take responsibility for everyone else. It started with my father and then my mother and siblings and with no understanding that *I could not be responsible for someone else's choices.*

It is important to understand you can only be responsible for *your* choices, behaviors and actions, not someone else's. And you are certainly not responsible for the results of someone else's actions.

If you are busy taking responsibility for the things you did not do and cannot control, you are leaving yourself short of time and energy to address the things you can control. In order to unshackle and reveal the remarkable within you, you must let go of the belief you can control other people. It cannot be done. To unshackle **Remarkable You,** focus on what *you* can control.

As John C. Maxwell, who is my mentor and friend and an internationally recognized leadership expert, speaker, coach, and author says, "The one thing all successful people have in common is that they take responsibility."

So what are we responsible for?

It starts with our own choices. Once we have the realization we make choices each and every day about our attitude, our behavior and how we treat ourselves and others, we can begin to change our lives. We start by identifying what choices serve us well and what choices do not serve us well.

As Eleanor Roosevelt said, "In the long run, we shape our lives and we shape ourselves. The process never ends until we die. And the choices we make are ultimately our own responsibility."

The choices we make every day make us **remarkable**!

Focus Points:

- Are you taking responsibility for things you cannot control?
- Are you blaming others for things you can control?

Action Steps for Your Journey:

- Take a moment to visualize how your life would improve, if you took responsibility for yourself and no one else.
- In your journal, write one thing you can start taking responsibility for right away.

Chapter 3

The Fundamental Need to Belong

As I discussed in Chapter 1, shame is the intensely painful feeling we are unworthy of belonging. As humans we are created biologically to be part of a group. The need to belong is in our DNA. That is why shame is so insidious: it taps into our deep, instinctive fear that comes with this need to belong: that we will die because we do not deserve to be part of the group.

Unfortunately for my mother, my siblings and me, shaming was part of our daily lives after my father's death. My sister Gail and I attended St Ursula's Catholic School in Armidale, a regional town which was a long bus ride away from our home. As you know, we already stood out as different at the school for all the wrong reasons. We had been taken into the school as part of their charity and we were provided with uniforms and food for lunch. We knew we did not belong there before our father killed himself.

On our first day back at school after those traumatic events, there was a whole school assembly. The sister-in-charge, who was leading the assembly, told the whole school Dad had committed suicide, a mortal sin. She singled us out for attention, she pointed to us and said I played a part in his death. In the Catholic faith, suicide is the worst sin. I was already feeling ashamed of who I was, because I had been told I was different and different was bad. Now the most important person at my school, a woman of standing in the community, an authority figure, publicly told me, I was part of the sin.

They told me God would judge me, and send me to burn in the fires of hell for killing my father. Even though I was attending a Catholic school I had not really thought much about God and this became my first real introduction to this God, this mean and angry God who would make me pay. What a burden to place on a child!

My mother coped with the pain and the shame by escaping into alcohol and drugs. Her drinking became worse, to the point she was not just drinking alcohol, but methylated spirits, a pure form of alcohol that can make you go blind, or kill you. She also started taking a morphine drug Dad used for the pain of his bowel cancer. Back then you could buy it over the counter at the chemist if you signed the poison register. She started off buying from the little chemist in Uralla, but after a while she sent Gail and me to different places to buy it for her. We walked many miles, little knowing what we were doing was enabling her addiction.

If you are reading this, and recognizing those emotions and behaviors, hear my heart: you are not worthless. Whatever shame you feel, for whatever reason, you are worthy of love and belonging. We all are. In those dark days I am not sure I would have believed those words if someone had said them to me, but they are the truth. Each one of us is remarkable in our own unique way, and we all have our place in the world. We all belong.

My mum's drinking and her inability to care for her children brought us to the attention of the authorities again—the Department of Child and Social Welfare, as it was known at the time, were already aware of us due to Mum and Dad's drinking habits. Only two months after Dad's funeral, Mum was admitted to hospital for taking an overdose of sleeping pills, and we kids were placed in foster care.

After that Mum was under constant watch. Relatives reported her every move to our assigned case worker, who visited our home many times after Dad died. The case worker's notes, which my brother obtained through what is now known as the Department of Family and Community Services when I started to write this story, said Mum "could not be left on her own during the day but had the children with her at night to look after her."

How often do we think we have imagined the circumstances we had to face? After all, our minds can play tricks on us. Surely it could not have been that bad? I know I have heard some people say that when I have shared my story.

That case file has been a gift to me as it gave me confirmation of what I knew to be true. It also showed me that in many instances it was even worse than I remember. It showed me Mum tried and tried to conform to the expectations of the social welfare services and the people in those small regional towns. On balance, I can see the welfare case worker did try, in his own way, to help our family, but the file notes reflect a bias that would not be acceptable today. They also demonstrate authorities reinforced Mum's belief she was not fit to be a mother.

Mum's drinking and drug taking became excessive again. No matter how hard she tried, she could not stop. The case worker encouraged her to join Alcoholics Anonymous (AA), and introduced her to a friend of his from AA, a man who was much older than her, who I will call Mr Williams.

There is no doubt in my mind after reading the file the case worker intended for Mum to become Mr Williams' wife. Mum believed she could not be a good mother without a husband and, sadly, was encouraged to believe that by her case worker. I can only imagine the pressure she must have felt to remarry so she could keep her family together. One of the file notes said,

> Mrs Munsie is quite an attractive woman now, she is well dressed, clean and sober and has regained personal dignity and the prospects for her and the family now seem to be good. AA has been good to her and have kept in constant contact.

This was just a few months after Dad's death, but Mum thought Mr Williams loved her and he would be good for us children. Little did she realize he would be the absolute opposite of that. I am sure she must have felt she had no other choice but to marry Mr Williams, and this presented itself as a life line.

On 29 November 1966, six months after my dad's death, Mum married Mr Williams. The file noted the case worker went to the wedding:

> *Today I was present at the wedding of Mrs Munsie and Mr Williams at the Court House in Armidale and the blonde Mrs Munsie looked very charming in mist blue.*

Mr Williams moved us into a flat in Armidale. Things quickly became worse for Mum and for us. He would beat us and lock us in our rooms. It turned out he wanted my mum, not the kids who came with her. When the marriage was not what she imagined, Mum spiraled out of control again.

Mum was desperately trying to find a place to belong, instead she found false friends who only wanted to use her, and exploit her vulnerability. That is what we do when we feel unworthy: we look for approval from others. It is easy to fall for false friends when you are an outsider and you are looking for someone, anyone, to approve of you and accept you. It is such a strong human need to belong, we will do anything to feel part of a group.

Life in Armidale was not good for us at all. I simply do not have words to explain the beatings and the physical and mental abuse. My sister Gail and I started hanging out with the wrong crowd. A much older man hung around us, his son was part of the group. I understand now he was a pedophile. He would ask the girls to take their clothes off so he could take photos. He also tried to sexually assault us. Thank God, something told me to stay well away.

Reflection: False friends

When we feel unworthy, we become desperate for approval, for someone to tell us we are worthy. The more desperate we are, the less able we are to be discerning about whose opinion matters, and we can sometimes be willing to do anything to fit in. We feel we have to prove our worth, and there are many people who will take advantage of that.

The **Remarkable You** has no need to prove itself to anyone. It knows you are worthy and you, just like every other human, have a purpose.

Focus Points:

- Who are you trying to please, or prove yourself worthy to?
- Have you found yourself in the wrong crowd, knowing it is wrong but desperate to seek their approval?
- What would happen if you made a 1% shift from seeking approval of others to approving of yourself?

Action Steps for Your Journey:

- Take time to journal on something you are great at, so you start to see your own value.
- Write down some ways you can be your own best friend. Treat yourself as though you are worthy—you are!

Chapter 4

Numbing the Pain

At the time all this was happening, I believed I was responsible for Mum's pain, and it was my fault she had no hope. From where I sit now, at 65 years old and with much greater insight into how the pain of shame, loneliness and hopelessness affect us, it is so much clearer: Mum was taking the one way out she knew. She tried everything she could to numb her pain, and when it got too much, she tried to take her own life. I am sure she believed we would be better off without her, because she felt worthless.

By January 1967 my eldest sister Gail had run away from home. I took to wagging school and staying with my mum. Remember, I wanted to protect her. Whatever my mum needed I did, and she needed a drinking partner. When she had no one to drink with, she forced me to drink with her. There I was at 14 years old, drinking all the time, often to the point of passing out drunk. By April, it was out of control. Mum was back on the morphine, and I was never at school and often drunk.

Eventually, Mr Williams left. The case worker's report

says, "Poor Mr Williams has been landed with a ratbag wife and a parcel of children who should never have been his responsibility."

Carol, Shirley Kerri and Steven were all placed in a Catholic orphanage in Armidale, as 'neglected children'. I was left with my mum and life became even worse. There are so many heart-breaking stories from the time my siblings were in the orphanage, but they are not mine to share. I do not think I will ever forget how they begged us to take them home every time we visited.

My mum was drunk and depressed without her children and I could not make it better: she wanted all her children with her. She decided to go back to AA to get some help. You have a sponsor in AA who you contact when you think you will drink again; they are supposed to help you work the 12 steps of recovery and to resist temptation to drink. Once again, my mum's sponsor ended up having a relationship with her. I will call him Mr Marsh.

In my eyes this was a step up for Mum, and for me. Mr Marsh had a poultry farm outside of Tamworth, lived in a beautiful home, and cared for us both. Little did we know, he was already married with a wife and daughter living in Tamworth. Without remembering too many details, things became difficult and we moved with Mr Marsh to a flat in Birchgrove in Sydney (near Balmain). Mum stopped drinking and applied, over and over, for custody of my sisters and brother. Mum and I caught the train to Armidale, just the two of us, to go before the court. When they said no, as they did many times, we would catch the train back. Mum would be depressed and crying. She was so desperate to have all her family together.

One day we were at Chatswood Mall shopping center and I was sitting in Mr Marsh's car with Mum, and there, walking up the street, was my eldest sister Gail, with a man! I ran after her and when I reached her, she realized it was me. I remember my absolute joy. She had got her life on track and was engaged to be married. Finally, we knew she was okay. Our family was starting to come back together, or so I thought.

By then I was 15, working in a factory as an office assistant. I had so little education, I do not know how I got the job. I made a friend there who would become part of my saving grace. Mum was trying her best to be sober, but not always succeeding. Her relationship with Mr Marsh was starting to be rocky and he was absent from home much more. When he found a younger woman without children, he left my mother and the same old pattern repeated itself.

My father killed the pain with his gun; my mother with drugs and alcohol. She could not maintain sobriety, the addiction too strong. Mum was always drunk or so high on morphine she could not get out of bed. One day she was hallucinating and I was so frightened I rang an ambulance. She was admitted to hospital and her stomach was pumped.

As a result of me calling the ambulance, Mum was admitted to Cullan Park Psychiatric Hospital for treatment. The hospital told me to leave, that I could not help her, but I truly did not know what to do. The next day at work I confided in my friend. She said I could live with her family until I could find somewhere to live. My friends' parents helped me accept I could not help my mother. By the time Mum was released from the hospital, I was living in a youth hostel.

Reflection: Pain

Please remember: if reflecting on your pain puts you at risk with your emotions, seek support immediately to work it through.

Drugs and alcohol are a common way we numb the pain we feel. We can also do it with overeating, or starving ourselves; binge-watching too much TV or gaming every spare hour; excessive retail therapy; or having risky casual relationships. It is the reason behind the activity that is the issue.

We cannot change the past. The past can only hurt us now if we choose to let it. When we use self-destructive behaviors to avoid feeling the pain of our past, we are just creating more pain: in our present, and in our future ... and if we have children, or other loved ones, they may be the collateral damage.

Much of the pain we feel is linked to the shame, and the sense of worthlessness and hopelessness we feel. We can choose to change the *bogus stories* that cause those feelings. We can choose to see our past in the rear-view mirror, instead of giving it power in our present. It is the choices you make now and going forward that will reveal the gold ... the remarkable within you.

Focus Points:

To unshackle **Remarkable You**, start by identifying:

- what you do to distract you from, or numb painful feelings
- where you learned those behaviors
- what painful feelings you are avoiding. Do you know what you are afraid to feel?

Action Steps for Your Journey:

- Pick one unhealthy numbing behavior you can change, and journal about what you can do instead. If you binge on Netflix when you feel sad, for example, you might decide to go for a walk around the block instead.
- Commit to avoiding that behavior while you are reading this book. Maybe you can read this book instead of shopping. Making that choice is a great next step.

Chapter 5

The Downward Spiral

Everyone has a story and each story matters. I have shared in this book as much of my life as I felt the reader needed to hear to appreciate why I would need to search for hope. In this chapter, I am sharing what happens when you cannot find hope.

There is no question growth involves struggle, or an uphill climb. But the alternative to that uphill climb, is a downhill slide, or worse, a downward spiral. Negative thoughts and dark feelings like guilt and shame lead to destructive, unhealthy behaviors, which lead to more guilt, more shame and more self-loathing. That is what I witnessed in the last months of my mother's life and that is her tragic story. Do not let it become yours.

After Mum was released from the psychiatric hospital she was able to get follow-up support as an outpatient. She found work in a cheese cake factory and continued the treatment, and she started to see great improvement. She made another application to the courts and, at last, they said yes! In February 1970, Carol, Shirley Kerri and Steven were released back into her care. Mum was so happy—but the happiness was not to last.

Her attempts to stay off the drugs and alcohol could not be maintained. She relaxed her guard and as soon as something painful happened she fell back into the familiar, destructive behaviors. There was another man and when he left she started drinking heavily again.

She tried to work but struggled. She started taking the morphine drug again and would send us out to buy it from the chemist. There was no food, all the money went on alcohol and drugs. Carol, Shirley Kerri and Steven would steal, to get things to sell, so they could buy food and drugs for Mum. I tried to help: I would come and stay with them as they were living in absolute squalor, and buy food with the little money I earned. The ladies from a Salvation Army Church on the corner also tried to help out with food. Mum's desperation grew, and she started drinking methylated spirits again because that is all she could get her hands on.

Mum would bring many men back to the house, exposing my sisters and brother and myself to drunkenness, drugs and sexual abuse. Then, on 28 August 1970, Mum filled the house with sailors. I have no idea where they came from. I was not there that night, so I was not able to protect my sisters and brother.

That night my sister, Carol, was drugged and raped. After she refused alcohol, she was given a cup of tea by someone. She did not remember anything after that except feeling dizzy. She woke up on her bed, which was a mattress on the floor, and when she tried to get out of her room, discovered she was locked in. Carol told me when Mum let her out, she was told one of the men "had drugged her and had sexual intercourse" (her words) with her. Our sister, Gail, encouraged Carol to report it to the police, and on 2 September 1970, detectives came to the house to investigate. In the police report is a detailed description of a horrific scene of filth. It is like reading a fiction story, except it was our life.

The police report said "The house was filled with filthy clothing, empty beer cans and the toilet floor covered in vomit." It goes on, "The room upstairs where Carol was assaulted was filled with filth, including a soiled mattress showing blood signs of the assault."

Once again, my sisters and brother were placed into foster care as neglected children. My mother loved us, and had put herself through all sorts of humiliation to have the younger children returned to her. She did not want this for Carol, or for the rest of us. I know this incident, and the events that followed while she was in care, affected Carol greatly. She became an alcoholic, which contributed to her early death. Sadly, she was not able to overcome the pain in her life.

In the Department of Community Services file on our family, there is a handwritten note from Mum where she is begging the welfare case worker to help her get Carol, Shirley Kerri and Steven back. Her mother's heart is so evident in her words and in her handwriting; I could hear her voice as I read. I saw her desperate desire for her to have her family together, but also her overwhelming grief.

My parents' example was when life is too much, the pain too great, take your own life. The impact of their choices fell to us, the generation that came behind them. Live or die: that is the choice, and they chose death. Hopelessness spirals us ever downwards towards this dark destination.

Six days after Carol, Shirley Kerri and Steven were taken from her, at the age of 38, my mother finally succeeded in taking her own life from a drug and alcohol overdose.

Mum was not found until late on 9 September, the day I turned 17.

My mother finally killed the pain in her life, but suicide is not the answer. It ends your painful life, yes, but it tragically impacts the lives of those closest to you.

Our lives are filled with choices and my mum and dad's choices were imposed on me, my sisters and my brother. We were set on a path to inherit a cookie cutter version of our parents' life, but I changed that destiny by discovering hope.

Reflection: Hopelessness

Both my mother and my father experienced hopelessness, and for many years I did too. That is why I believe in the power of hope. I understand only too well how damaging hopelessness is.

Hopelessness is commonly listed as a symptom for mental health problems including depression, post-traumatic stress disorder, substance dependency and suicide ideation. As my parents' lives demonstrated, all these things are often bound up together, and change seems impossible because ... where do you start? It seems too big and you feel too small.

If you are feeling hopeless right now, and perhaps a little angry with yourself, please do not be, that is just another *bogus story*. By reading this book, you have already taken the first steps into your journey, so I know you can do it! Together we will unshackle, reveal and enable the remarkable within you!

When we feel hopeless, we reinforce that feeling by telling ourselves things can never change: that is what hopelessness is really, the belief things can never be different. That is why it is important to watch your words—words have power.

As the wise prophet Solomon said, "Words kill, words give life; they are either poison or fruit—you choose." As you take this journey be aware of your words: both the thoughts in your head and the words that come out of your mouth.

Focus Points:

- Is there an area of your life where you feel hopeless, or do you feel everything is hopeless?
- Do you think, or say things like: "my situation will never get better," "I feel like giving up," "It is hopeless," or "nothing will ever change?"

Action Steps for Your Journey:

- Identify the words you are using to describe yourself and your situation, in your thoughts, in your speech and in your writing: emails, messages, chat. Notice when you criticize yourself, call yourself names, or tell yourself you or your situation is awful, useless, hopeless.
- Take time over the next few days to increase your awareness of these words and think about how you can start to rephrase them. Use your journal to record things you say over and over to yourself. These 'tapes' needed to be recorded over with new data!

For example:
Instead of "This situation will never get better," try "I will not always be in this situation."
Instead of "I give up," try "I will try something different."

Chapter 6

A Vision of Hope

After Mum was admitted to the psychiatric hospital, my friend's family took me in for a while, and helped me find a place in a Catholic youth hostel in Strathfield. They were very kind and encouraged me to accept I could not fix things for my mother.

In the hostel with other girls—mean girls, I soon found out—I was once again made aware I was different. On the first day, I was shown to a bed in the dorm room, and the first girl who spoke to me said, "What is wrong with you, don't you shave under your arms?" I had been judged by someone else's standards and they reinforced I was different and unacceptable.

There was another lesson on this life journey right there in this hostel. I was 16 years old, carrying emotional baggage, starting a life I knew nothing about in a hostel of young dysfunctional girls. Young girls that were not averse to bullying anyone that was different and I was different. Different was bad, I knew that! Those girls reinforced that belief in me with their words and actions.

Even though I was not living at home full time, I would

go and stay with my mum and my siblings regularly in the months before her death. On my way to one of these visits, I had a vision that has stayed with me all these years.

I remember it so clearly, even to the point of what I was wearing. I was sitting on the bus on the way to their flat and, as usual, I was pretending to be someone else, because who I was could never be enough. I had on a black and white floral dress.

Out of the blue, came this vision: a waking dream, a picture in my mind of what my life would be. I saw a woman of influence: a woman standing in front of a room full of people, and when she spoke, people listened, and lives were changed. I could see it so very clearly and I knew, deep within my heart, it was me! It was a vision of the future, of what I could become.

How could this be? My rational brain dismissed the thought as simply a daydream. Everything I experienced, everything the world told me I was, convinced me that future would be impossible for me. My circumstances would stop me. I had little education and I was destined for the same life as my parents, I was certain.

But deep inside me, even then, on that bus, in that moment there was something different, something better for me ... but I had no idea how to find it.

Reflection: Hope

Hope is such a simple word and yet it means so much to anyone going through a difficult time. Hope can be the difference between keeping going and giving up.

We all have the capacity for hope within us, just as we have the capacity for hate and anger. Hope is a seed we get to water or to kill: it is a choice!

Hope is not something we can purchase and add to our lives. It is not something we can get from other people. We need to find the hope within ourselves.

If your hopes have ever been dashed, you will be familiar with the shadow side of hope. That is when we tie our worth and happiness to things being a certain way. It is tinged with fear because we know deep inside we cannot control how things will turn out. True hope, the hope I want to help you discover, is the belief we are remarkable and can aspire to reach our highest potential.

Do not pin your hopes on a specific outcome in the future like "I will be an Opera Singer" or "I will lose weight." You are remarkable *now*, in the present. Your potential is the greatest you can possibly become: how deep that vein of gold is within you. That is the story you get to write of your life, with the choices you make every day. Hope is the belief you always have the choice to step into that potential.

I like to use **HOPE** as an acronym:

Hanging
On with
Patient
Expectation.

When we feel hope*less,* we cannot see any way out of our current circumstances. The things we need seem out of our reach: not material things or comforts, but human needs like belonging and love. What my journey to hope showed me is, we do not need to know exactly how our lives will change, we just need to have faith they will and, whenever possible, water the seed of hope by making positive choices that serve the remarkable within us.

Focus Points:

• Have you been waiting for someone or something to give you hope for your future?
• Have your hopes focused on having things a certain way?
• Was there a time when you believed you could achieve your true potential?

Action Steps for Your Journey:

• Sift through your story for a time when you believed you could aspire to your highest potential or saw a glimpse of a deep passion or purpose within you.
• If there was a time you believed you could achieve your potential, write about how that felt, and what stopped that belief.
• If you have never believed you could achieve your potential, write about what it would be like to believe you could. What new possibilities would open up?

Chapter 7

The Bogus Stories in our Baggage

The example my parents showed me was that when the pain was too much the answer was to take your own life. We repeat as adults what we saw others do when we were children, and the impact of the actions of those others that are family or close loved ones imprints on us more than we realize.

How I survived growing up is a miracle and it is only as I have looked back in the rear-view mirror of my life that I have seen this.

After Mum died, the guilt kicked in again. I should have stayed; I could have kept her alive; she died on her own; and I was supposed to look after her. What had I done? On top of the burden I was already carrying over my father's death, I layered the burden of Mum's death.

As I have already discussed in early chapters, the dark feelings of guilt and shame made me think negatively about myself and my opportunities: dismissing the vision of hope, for example. The dark feelings and negative thoughts spurred 'bad' behaviors.

In the year after my mother's death, this played

out as me continually seeking the approval of others. An old pattern of behavior from when I was younger re-emerged. I always imagined I was someone else and tried to be like someone else, because someone else was always better than me. That was my way of seeking approval: I wanted to be loved and needed, I wanted to fit into someone else's life because after all, their life *had* to be better than mine.

We do this, don't we? We look at what someone else has and think, "I want that." We look at all the external things that seem to prove they are better than us and we think if we can make our outside like their outside, we will be better too. We mimic their behavior, perhaps adopting language, or habits. At times, we even dress like them because there is such a deep-down desire for approval. But all we can be is the very best version of who we are!

My journey through this season of my life was difficult, because everything I did and saw was filtered through my guilt and shame—and a very nasty attitude. I believed the world owed me something. I was bitter, angry and resentful and this was in every action I took and every word I spoke. It was completely entrenched in every part of me.

I moved out of the hostel and privately boarded in many homes and I am grateful for the kind people who did their best to speak into my life and try to help me. But in my mind I was way past help by then. Just like my parents, my life was spinning out of control and every time something went wrong, I had to fight off the urge to take my own life.

We seek and search but, until we have an awareness of what we are looking for, we seek the wrong thing. There were many people coming in and out of my life. Some good people and some not so good. We can often attract into our inner circle those that are like-minded and I was doing that for some time, attracting and being attracted to people with the same 'world owes me' attitude and negative thinking that had become my habit.

In 1972, just before my 18th birthday, I married for the first time. I met a young man who lived opposite where I was boarding in a private home. The story I told myself was I needed to be loved (without even knowing the first thing about what love was), and I needed someone to look after me. The day we married I cried all day knowing full well it was wrong, but at that point I did not know how to stop it. I brought all my baggage: shame, guilt, suicidal tendencies and addictions into that marriage. Nothing had been dealt with, not even really identified, and I did not even know who I really was. I had such a limited awareness of who 'Wendy' was and why I felt like I did. It certainly was not a healthy way to start a marriage.

When we carry our toxic baggage into situations, as I did into this marriage, it poisons everything we touch. Our marriage was not a happy place. I was in full flight going down the same path as my parents: drinking heavily to numb the pain, fighting because of the pain, and having constant thoughts of suicide. I was letting the generational pattern, and my belief that it was my destiny, become my reality.

In this place, this unhappy marriage, we had a son. That was a joyful moment but sadly our marriage got worse and I ended up leaving when I was pregnant with our daughter. Two precious gifts from this marriage: my son and daughter. But at the time I left, my husband refused to let me have our son. He took him and went to live with his mother.

Eventually I met someone else, and guess what? I was still carrying that baggage. I carried with me all my shame, guilt, suicidal tendencies and addictions with me, everywhere I went.

When we carry something for a long time our arms ache and it seems heavier than when we started out. It is the same with the baggage we carry in our hearts and minds: unless we can put them down, they weigh us down. Just like when we travel on a holiday, we pick up souvenirs along the way, well it is the same in life. As I traveled through life I souvenired more things to add to my baggage. My first marriage failed so I added extra servings of guilt to the burden of this baggage. How I behaved was not okay, my drinking was not okay, my thoughts were horrible and the guilt unbearable, but I had no idea what to do.

In 1977, when I married my husband Bill, a good man, I became part of a family that had everything I had never experienced. They were stable, and they loved and deeply cared for each other. They tried their best to embrace me into their family, but I struggled tremendously. They may have never known this, but in my mind the battle was fierce. I knew I did not fit in. My image of who I was did not fit with this family: a family who loved for and cared for each other; a family which spoke words of encouragement and love to each other; a family which was way out of my reach, so I thought. Often no one knows what is going on in our minds except us. All others see is the outer-workings of this internal drama and battle through our attitude and consequent behavior. Remember: people feel your attitude even before you open your mouth.

In the early days, my marriage to Bill was filled with good, bad and ugly moments. There were many battles in that time and my addictions were getting worse: I was drinking heavily. Admittedly, the group we hung around with were very big drinkers, so perhaps I did not stand out, but I knew deep inside of me it was not okay.

We had two children together and as our family grew, so did my pain, shame and guilt, and all that went with these feelings. My thoughts of suicide were out of control. Whenever something went wrong—when I got hurt by someone, or when it all seemed too hard—the solution my parents taught me presented itself: take my own life. I kept thinking my family would be better off without me and my husband's family, whose life looked great to me, could look after them.

The insidious thing about shame and guilt, is we do not tell anyone what we are thinking and feeling: we carry it inside us. Often those looking into our lives will never know the *bogus stories* we are carrying around with us, and are making us feel hopeless and unworthy. We cannot possibly admit the darkness of our hearts and minds to anyone, because we believe if we do, we will find out for sure how worthless we are. That is another *bogus story*, one that sets us up for a life fraught with desperation, without the self-awareness to know we need help. The ending to these *bogus stories* can often be tragic: another person lost to suicide. That is where I was heading and, sadly, those closest to me would have never known.

Reflection: Bogus Stories

Bogus stories are untruths you believe about yourself. Our brains love stories. We use stories to help us understand the world, and our place in it, without even realizing we are doing it. The trouble is, we are not always very good at telling the difference between a true, helpful story and a bogus, destructive story.

Bogus stories can come from our circumstances, from what people have spoken about us and even from the lies we have told ourselves. *Bogus stories* often come in the form of other people's negative opinions of us. Too often in life we let someone else's negative opinion become our truth.

Even though we do not like the *bogus stories,* they can become part of our identity; we talk about them and live in that space. These *bogus stories*, the shame, the guilt, the untruths are familiar when we have lived in that space for a long time. They feel safe because they are familiar. Sadly without taking an intentional action to move out of that space, living those *bogus stories*, you can find yourself stuck. But you can move into new unfamiliar territory with intentional action!

Words carry power: the power to build us up or tear us down. Once we start to believe these *bogus stories*, we look for proof: words and events that confirm them, and guess what? We find what we look for.

Focus Points:

- Opinions are the cheapest commodities in the world. Where have you allowed someone else's opinion of you, their *bogus story*, to become your truth?
- What *bogus stories* are holding you back from what you want?
- When have you collected those *bogus stories* and added them to the daily baggage you carry?

Action Steps for Your Journey:

- Start by identifying the things you know are *bogus stories*, those untruths that have become part of your identity.
- In your journal, argue against those stories.

For example, if someone in your life told you that you are lazy, even though you work hard, you might write:

Bogus story: I am lazy.

The truth: I work hard every day: I go to work, cook all the meals, and do all the laundry. I reject that *bogus story*.

If you are numbing your pain with alcohol, you might write something like this:

Bogus story: I am a drunk.

The truth: I drink too much, but I can change that behavior, and there is more to me than just my drinking.

Chapter 8

The Seed of Hope

The biggest *bogus story* in my head was I was worthless. I kept trying to attach myself to someone who could make me better, make life better for me. Sadly, we cannot ask someone else to change us, it must start with us.

Somehow, in my very worst, most desperate moments in those early years of my marriage to Bill, that vision of myself as a woman of influence came back to me, and would not leave me alone. That vision was my seed of hope.

That seed of hope triggered something deep inside of me, and I started to believe there could be a different life, a different way forward than alcoholism and suicide. Perhaps it was looking at my children and worrying they would all go down the same path as me and as my parents. My three sisters and brother were already on the same path: could I avoid passing on this inheritance?

How could I make a change? What would I do? How could I find what change looked like? What was hope for me and my family? The addictions and suicidal tendencies were stronger than ever. I had to fight something inside me every time they came. I do not entirely know why I did not give in to them, but I am so very thankful I did not.

I started to go to a little Anglican Church near our home, a tiny place with about 20 people in the congregation. At the time I did not know what motivated me to go but I did, and I took our three children with me.

I think I saw this as a way forward for my children—not for me, I was past help. Remember, my image of God was the image of a cruel and vengeful judge who would burn me in the fires of hell; but my husband's family attended the Anglican Church where they lived, to get married in and to have their children christened. We had had our children christened there too.

So I started attending this church with the children but nothing really changed. I was still the same confused, mixed up young woman, and many times I turned up very hungover for their services. Even though it was in a small town, they did not seem to know much about me. The people there were nice to me and did not treat me like an outsider.

I just love when we take a step, or have even a tiny thought in the right direction, something happens to support us to follow that path: someone or something comes along at the perfect time to give us what we need. By taking the small step of going to that church, I watered my seed of hope, I opened up new possibilities for myself, and in August 1986 something happened that helped me change my path.

I had been attending this church on and off and, like I

said previously, nothing had really changed in how I felt or in my behavior, but one day, one of the dear women from this church invited me to see a special guest speaker at a different church. I immediately said no: why would I want to do that? Why on earth would I need to do that!

I had absolutely no intention of going, but at the last moment something in me told me to go. It was a whole new experience for me. I could not tell you what the speaker said but, at the end, he asked people who wanted their life to change to come out the front. Let me tell you I was first out of my seat!

That feeling deep down inside me, the belief there had to be something better, kicked in with such force I could not stop myself walking out the front, even though I had no idea what to expect. In that moment I had a choice and I made it: I wanted change, so I would do something different.

In life we often find ourselves in a defining moment: a moment in time when we get to choose which way we will go and our choice in that moment will define our future. These moments happen more than once in our lives. This was one of those for me, a moment that defined my future.

As I stood out the front of that congregation, a woman came up to me. I think I expected her to talk to me and ask what was wrong. She did not even ask me my name. She just touched my arm and prayed for me.

The lady that stood there praying, said she had a word from God for me. "Sure", you might be thinking: I know that is what I thought. I was shaking, expecting any message from God would be the one that was going to send me to burn in the fires of hell for killing my dad, but this is what she said, "God knows the guilt you have carried over your father's death. It was not your fault."

I did not know this woman, I had never seen her before. I had never told anyone, even those closest to me, what happened. Not even my husband knew how I felt or even the whole story about my dad. No one, absolutely no one, knew what was in my heart. Why would I share that with anyone? This woman certainly did not know. I had never seen her before and have never seen her since.

God knows the guilt you have carried over your father's death. It was not your fault.

Those words impacted me so profoundly, they went deeply into every area of my mind and heart. I was sobbing! Someone knew how I felt! Someone, this God, knew what happened! Maybe I was not going to hell after all.

The woman then asked if I wanted to accept Jesus into my heart. I did not know what that meant, but if this Jesus knew my guilt, I was saying yes, and I did.

Please as you read this, hear my heart. I did not understand what happened to me in those moments, but something happened, and for the first time, I felt that speck of hope. Yes, it was a very tiny seedling, but it was there.

This was not a magical transformation, if that is what you are thinking. I went home to the same situation that night and woke up in the same circumstances the next morning. What I did wake up to was a slight lifting of the guilt I had carried for almost 20 years.

Reflection: Powering hope

What are you giving power to in your life?

We tend to block out the horror in our lives in the hope it is not real. I know from experience there is a need to face the fears of the past, because if our past is fully dead, it cannot affect our future. Letting go of the guilt over my father's death was an important step in setting me on the path to the future. Instead of giving power to the *bogus stories* that dragged me down, I was free to empower the vision of that 16 year old girl, that dream I could be a women of influence. I was able to give intention to the vision by thinking about it, and speaking it out. I was able to attach myself to hope for the future.

We get to decide every day what we empower. As John C Maxwell said, "Where there is no hope in the future, there is no power in the present."

Do you want to be a historian, always focusing on how bad your past was, never appreciating the things you do have? It is hard to find that dream, that hope, if you are constantly looking backwards into your past because if your head is turned backwards, while you are trying to walk forward, you will trip over. But if you look back, as if you are looking through a rear-view mirror only, your eyes will be forward, looking toward and walking into the future.

Do you want to be a reporter, always telling everyone how bad your current situation is and how it can never change? That was me: I was in my 'whine zone'—always complaining about how bad life was and taking no responsibility.

Somewhere deep inside of you, you have a dream, a vision of what your future could look like, should look like. It is time to bring that alive. Become a futurist: keep traveling with me on this journey, focusing on the great future ahead and doing what you can to create the future you want, and deserve.

The only power the past has over you is the power you choose to give it. Your hope is in the future and you have the power in the present to create your future!

It is time to power your hope, and turn your life around. Are you ready?

Focus Points:

- What you agree with, you empower; what you empower, devours you—what have you empowered from your past that you are allowing to devour your future?
- How are you giving power to hopelessness? Are you a historian? A reporter? Both?

Action Steps for Your Journey:

- In your journal, write out your truth. The REAL truth of who you are: who you would be if you achieved your highest potential. That will be the seed of your hope. If you do not know what else to write, write this:

I am remarkable.

Write it 10 times, then write some thoughts on how your attitude and behavior would be different if you believed that truth. For example, I would write, over and over, I am a woman of influence. Then I would think about what my attitude and behaviors would look like if I was a woman of influence. What behaviors served that potential? What behaviors needed to change?

Chapter 9

Becoming a Futurist

So there I was, the next morning after this revelation that someone—this God I saw as something to be feared—knew the guilt I carried about my dad's death and said it was not my fault! What was I to do with this information? I had no idea, but somewhere in my turmoiled heart I had the beginnings of true hope.

Up until then I blamed everyone, starting with myself, for everything that happened from the day Dad died and my uncle Ted sexually assaulted me. I took responsibility for the wrong things and failed to take responsibility for myself.

If I was not to blame and this higher power I had been so fearful of, was not going to throw me into the pit of hell, what did that mean? What was I meant to do?

That day, for the first time since those horrific events, I got angry. Not the unfocused anger I had for the world, but specific anger directed at the people who hurt me: Dad and Mum and Uncle Ted. I got angry at my dad who asked me to hand him his gun, and I was angry I had carried the blame and guilt, for something I did not do, for way too long. I got angry at Mum, who did not protect me from my uncle, exposed me to abuse and forced me to participate in her drinking bouts. I got angry at Uncle Ted: how dare he take my vulnerability and exploit it to fulfill his sick urges. I was angry, really angry!

In these defining moments of our lives, many thoughts can come flooding into our minds and that is certainly what happened for me. I needed to sift through my thoughts to find out what was real and what was not. The thoughts of shame and guilt were still there and needed to be worked through, and the addictions and suicidal tendencies still existed. Deep, deep down in the pit of my gut this uncontained anger was finally burning. But, undeniably, I also felt hope.

That morning, I noticed the chink of belief that things could get better, I could have a different future from my present, my parents' legacy was not my destiny. Little did I know then that watering this seed of hope to make it grow, would be the force that would be the catalyst for change.

Let me just state here: *it does not matter what your past is.* It does not matter what you have or have not done, it does not matter what your circumstances are, and it certainly *does not matter how old you are.*

No matter what, your situation is not hopeless!

What does matter are the choices we make when these defining moments come along: which path do we choose? One step begins a journey. With that first step of going to the church, and the second step of going to see the speaker, so I began my journey. Step by step over the next 12 months of my life I made small choices differently, and that started to shift things inside me, and in my life. It was not a straightforward journey: things did not magically fall into place.

Our landscape changed dramatically. My husband Bill lost his job and found work in Queensland, so we moved. We lost our home through bankruptcy in this period as well. But those losses: of our home, of the environment we lived in, of those people who played important roles in my journey to find hope … those losses taught me hope is something we need to find within ourselves. Sure, there are people, good people who will walk alongside us in our journeys if we will allow them, but remember: *hope is an inside job*. We cannot get it from someone else.

I also learned sometimes for internal change to take place, so we can see ourselves as remarkable, sometimes the external circumstances of our lives need to change: where we live, where we go, and who we allow to speak into our lives.

Being out of that environment, away from the influence of heavy drinkers who would never have thought to challenge me on my behavior or actions, I started to see more clearly. Hear my heart: I am not blaming someone else for who I was, or what I did, but once I stepped out of that environment, I saw a little more clearly.

I knew if I did not take this opportunity to take responsibility for myself, and stop looking for someone else to change me or fix me, I would end up the same as my parents and so would my children, and so every day I started to make choices that served my future, not the *bogus stories* of my past.

Reflection: Choices

When you make the choice to step in the right direction, sometimes even the smallest step becomes the biggest step in your life. When we are desperate for change and finally realize *it is us who need to make the change*, then our journey has really begun.

As I said earlier, we each have a free will choice, but until this point in my story I honestly did not realize this. It was such revelation for me, and it changed my life!

As a futurist, you are now focused on the possibilities in the future, but it is the choices you make every day that will make you! As Abraham Lincoln said, "You cannot escape the responsibility of tomorrow by evading it today."

We can choose to give power to hopelessness, by making choices that let the past influence our present, and create a future without hope, or we can choose to power our hope by making choices that enable the remarkable within.

It is time to **ACT**

A – decide what **action** you will take

C – identify what **choices** you will make

T – commit to a **time-frame** for this change

Focus Points:

- If you have been journaling as you go, you may have already been making positive changes. If so, well done! If not, what is stopping you?
- Where do you need to say *"no"* for your situation to change?
- Where do you need to step forward and say *"yes"* and make a choice for life to be different on this journey?

Action Steps for Your Journey:

- Identify one action you can make today that will step you toward the future you desire. Take that action.
- Write the choices you need to make in your journal, along with the timeline for making this change. Focus on things you *can* control.

For example:
Instead of writing "Lose weight" write "Stop eating chocolate bars for the next month."

It is never too late to start but it is always too late to wait!

Chapter 10

A Change of Attitude

We can become a victim of our circumstances, as I had, and this can come because of the actions of others. It started for me with the loss of my innocence through the actions of my parents and uncle; it will be different for each one of us. But the outcome is usually the same: a victim tends to believe hope, and a way forward, has to come from the actions of others.

I believed I was a victim for way too long, and the more we feel like that victim, the more we find all the circumstances to confirm we are a victim: what we search for, we find.

Over this period of years, Bill and I had two more children together, and we moved to Queensland after he lost his job and our landscape changed. We were in a new State and I knew no one except the wife of one of Bill's friends. Again I did not fit in. Life continued for us, as it does: in marriage, family and work. I was trying to prove my worth, but my shame was so entrenched and deep-rooted within me, it seemed I was continually reminded of my unworthiness as a wife and mother. I loved, and still love, all my children but, like my mum, I never felt like I was a good mum.

By then our home was not a happy place. I know I did not make it easy for Bill. I always felt like a failure. I would lay awake at night reminding myself of how and when I had failed, and envisioning how I would take my life, that was still my out. My search for this greater being, the God who knew I was not to blame, was amid it all, but I did not know who I was meant to be, or how I could feel worthy.

When you blame yourself and, deep down, blame the world for your lot in life, the victim attitude starts to seep out of your pores, just like garlic does when we eat too much. This victim attitude, seeps out in your words and actions, tainting everything you touch.

In my case this played out as me not caring about the impact my actions and words had on someone else. I felt the impact of others words on me, I had not thought too much about how my words and actions affected others.

My attitude was very nasty and presented itself in me as anger, bitterness and a resentful heart. We can use many things to numb ourselves against the painful feelings we have: as you know, my parents had tried to kill their pain by what they put in their mouths. Well, I was using my attitude as one of my pain killers.

What we agree with, we empower; what we empower devours us. My past was still devouring me at a very fast rate, and it needed to stop. I needed to do an about-face to enable my possible future to empower me instead of the past. I needed to be able to look in the mirror and see hope and potential and not hopelessness, failure, shame and guilt—otherwise what example was I setting for my children? The victim attitude was not working for me, and it had to go. Realizing this was such a light-bulb moment for me.

Remember, back then I was a 'control freak'. I realized the one thing I had control over was my attitude. I decided to enter a 'no whining zone' and develop an 'attitude of gratitude'. Please stay with me here: I know we can feel cynical when we hear people tell us to be grateful. What I mean by that is, I decided *I would look for something good instead of something bad.* I would train myself to think hope*full*y about a situation, instead of hope*less*ly. Doing this enabled me to build within myself a different set of habits and thought patterns.

It took me way too long to work out we have the power to make a choice about our attitude every day. Sometimes it is the only choice we will have on that day, in that moment, in the circumstances we face. We cannot change our past, and I know this so well, nor can we change how people act towards us and we cannot always change our circumstances in any given moment. *But* we *can* choose our attitude!

"Sure," you may think, "that is way too simple" and it seems like it is. If you have had a 'stinky' attitude for a long time, it is hard work to change it, but when you choose your attitude, you are taking control of your life, rather than just letting life control you. That is what I did. No more could I whine and wait for the actions of others to make something good happen.

As I have walked through my life, I have seen time and again the power of attitude on my life, as well as how it impacted on those in my sphere of influence. Yes, our families, friends and work colleagues are affected by our attitude. It has become very important to me because I know how my bad attitude colored my thoughts and preceded my actions.

Where we can go wrong is thinking that *attitude is a guarantee of happiness*. Let me tell you it is not! If I had to rely on being happy to have a good attitude, then I would have failed dismally. My attitude was not always good, it was a work in progress, but my attitude was not dependent on my happiness.

Attitude was simply a choice I made, despite what I felt inside. I could no longer pin my hopes and desires on someone or something else. It was mine, and mine alone, to control. Wow, this was such a mind shift for me! At last, I was no longer a victim.

Reflection: Attitude

"Attitude is the difference maker! Attitude isn't everything but it is the one thing that can make a difference in your life."

John C Maxwell

Choosing our attitude about the situations we find ourselves in enables us to see future circumstances in a different light. That is what it did for me and it was such a game changer. Our attitude colors our perspective both in the now and for the future. Our attitude cannot stop our feelings, but it can keep our feelings from stopping us.

Attitude precedes and colors everything you do, say and how you behave. Attitudes start in our hearts and minds and then come out of our mouths. Before we even speak, those around us: in our homes, in our jobs, in our communities, feel our attitude, and that can have enormous impacts.

My attitude played such a major role in me feeling angry, and like a victim. I felt trapped by my circumstances until I realized I could choose my attitude.

Once you realize the power of attitude, you can see circumstances and events differently, and change how you respond to them. After I cultivated an attitude of gratitude, I soon noticed the difference. I finally understood that people hear our words, but feel our attitude. As former US President Thomas Jefferson said, "Nothing can stop the man with the right mental attitude from achieving his goal; nothing on earth can help the man with the wrong mental attitude."

Focus Points:

• Where have you allowed your attitude to take control over how you behave and react?
• How has your attitude played a role in your thinking?
• When has your attitude been dysfunctional and how has this affected the way other people perceive you, and react to you?

Action Steps for Your Journey:

• Look back at what you wrote in your journal when you recorded your thoughts about what attitudes and behaviors would best serve the **Remarkable You.**
• Decide on how you will change your attitude, even one step at a time, but be intentional! If you have no other ideas, try my 'no whining' experiment. Simply catch yourself when you want to complain, whether out loud or in your head. Observe what difference a change of attitude makes over a week.

Chapter 11

Growing Belief in Yourself

The realization I had to opt into my life, take responsibility for me and stop allowing the past to control me was a major step on the journey. Up until then, I had given the events of the past way too much power but—let me say it again—the only power the past has over us is the power we choose to give it.

I still could not work out why, but I was no longer prepared to say this was 'my lot in life' and accept that alcoholism, struggle and suicide was all that was available to me. That seed of hope had germinated and it was starting to poke its little head up.

What did 'taking responsibility for me' look like? Until then I had allowed my circumstances and history to control me. Even though I did not like it, it was familiar and therefore safe and comforting in its own way. We do that, you know, we get caught up and we stay with what is familiar because it is easier, even when it is not serving us well, but as author Stephen Pressfield said, "It is one thing to lie to ourselves, it is another to believe it"—I had believed it, but would no more.

I had wanted to control others and those things around me, but I was not taking control of myself. The idea I could control myself was a new concept to me, but as I changed my attitude, I realized I could change other things too.

The number one catalyst for change is *action*. Controlling myself meant controlling my actions. I worked out that taking responsibility for me meant *action for me.* It meant no longer being prepared to choose the comfort of the patterns I knew, but to **act** to create new patterns. I now understand how action changes lives ... but all I knew then was I needed to focus on *my* actions. I knew for certain my step-by-step way forward would have to be *my* steps; they could not be someone else's.

I worked out my self-esteem could not come from others: it needed to come from within me. I needed to see myself as worthy, and self-worth was something I needed to earn for myself and confirm in myself every day on this journey of a thousand steps. This was about the reputation I had with myself.

It was all so new to me but something deep inside me told me I had one chance to break the mold I was born into, and drove me forward. I knew if I wanted things to be different for my children, my grandchildren and those who came behind me, then I could not pull back. I decided this new awareness of responsibility and accountability to myself, and for myself, needed to be at the forefront of what I did.

No way am I going to say it was easy—it was hard work—but I decided I was up for it. I changed my drinking habits: occasionally I would drink over dinner with friends, but it was not like it was in the past, I was no longer drinking to wipe myself out. I also stopped shopping to buy something new, to fulfill the desire to be accepted by what I wore or look liked. As time passed I really started to believe life could be different, and as I made changes for me, I started to see and feel a sense of self-worth.

Reflection: Being accountable

"The most important opinion you have is the one you have of yourself, and the most significant things you say all day are the things you say to yourself."
Author Unknown

Self-worth, self-respect and *self-esteem* cannot come from others, they need to come from within yourself. I can tell you we are all worthy, and each of us are remarkable, but if you do not believe in yourself, your brain will counter with all the reasons you are not worthy. If you are like me, you will have done things you are ashamed of, so you will be inclined to believe you are not worthy.

The solution starts with being consistently accountable to yourself for the choices you make. What does that mean?

It means making commitments to yourself, and sticking to them. It means being honest with yourself. It means forgiving yourself for the times you have let yourself down, and a new concept of counting on yourself to make those right choices.

This is when actions and patterns change and you learn you *can count on yourself*. It can help to have an accountability partner, perhaps a coach or a mentor, but it always starts as an inside job, an action inside our hearts and minds. When we start to feel good about ourselves on the inside, it gets easier and easier to make good choices for ourselves.

Focus Points:

- What areas in your life have you had no accountability for your actions and behaviors?
- What do you notice about the pattern you have identified?
- What triggers the bad choices ... is it certain people, or circumstances?

Action Steps for Your Journey:

- Pick an area where you have let yourself down in the past, and use ACT to plan a new pattern. If, for example, you know you always drink after you hand your kids over to your ex, make a plan to go walking with a friend, exchange the wine for a cup of tea or cook yourself a favorite meal instead.
- Consider if you need help on this stage of your journey such as a coach or accountability partner. Make that part of your action plan.

It is time to **ACT**

A – decide what **action** you will take

C – identify what **choices** you will make

T – commit to a **time-frame** for this change

Chapter 12

Choosing the people around you

The biggest key to discovering the remarkable Wendy within me, was learning to lead myself well. Taking responsibility for me: taking control of my attitude and my destructive behaviors, and being accountable to myself, were essential steps on my journey to discovering the remarkable within me. As I have said already, this journey is an inside job, the discovery comes from within … but we can find good people to walk alongside us for a season.

When I changed my attitude, it changed how I felt, how I acted and how I thought. I learned by choosing my attitude, it was easier for me to choose my actions. You may be thinking easier said than done, but remember: it is one step, then another step, then another and eventually we start to notice things look completely different.

Up to this point I had been in and out of jobs. I had gone to the College of Technical and Further Education (TAFE) when I was 17 to do secretarial studies, but I was not too good at shorthand and I failed. I was not afraid of hard work, and I worked whatever job I could get: a waitress, working in a factory and even delivering mail, because that is all I thought I was capable of. We can spiral into our very own self-defeating prophesy, looking at others and thinking we can never be good enough to do what they do.

I went from job to job until I found myself a role in a school as a teacher's aide. By then my attitude had taken a major turn for the better, and these people did not know the 'Old Wendy'. They only saw the potential in the woman they saw in front of them. For me, it was like I had a blank page for my life and I got to write on it.

I am grateful and thankful for this period in my life, which was a major growth period for me, and to the group of women at that school: the lovely teachers who championed me to be all I was meant to be. I doubt they realize the profound impact they had on my life.

Remember, I had very little post-school education. My only experience had been failure at TAFE in my secretarial studies, so I very much doubted my capacity to achieve. The people in this school saw something in me that up until then I did not even see myself. They became my cheer squad.

This is a perfect example of the power of our inner circle. Our inner circle is about who we allow close to us, to speak into our lives. A negative inner-circle will bury the remarkable within: a positive inner circle will empower it by helping us to see more than we can see ourselves. As John C Maxwell says, "Growth thrives in conducive surroundings." My new environment was conducive for growth—my growth.

Over this period I discovered that I had an ability to learn and to educate myself in ways I had never thought possible. Better still, I could apply what I learned. I realized I was great at encouraging and equipping others with my words and actions, whether it was students or the teachers I worked with. I discovered I was great at leadership. Who would have thought? Sometimes we get so caught up in who we are not, that we do not see who we really are, how remarkable we really are.

Nido Qubein, who arrived in the US as a teenager, with only $50 in his pocket, and became a hugely successful businessman once said, "Whether you are a success or a failure in life has little to do with your circumstances; it has much more to do with your choices.'" Changing my attitude, opting into my life and making choices that took me forward, made such a difference to my life. By making the choice to change my attitude, and making choices about my attitude every day, I put myself on a path into an environment I could not have imagined would welcome me, where I was surrounded by people who believed in me and encouraged me to grow.

I stayed in this school for nine years until these amazing women encouraged me to reach for more. They could see more in me, and for me. With their help I applied for, and secured, a great position in state government working in Human Resources on Workplace Health and Safety. It was really quite astonishing to me that I gained the position.

Reflection: Your inner circle

For a long time my inner circle were people who were like me: dysfunctional people who were also making bad choices and who would have never thought of calling out my behavior. We attract, and are attracted to, like-minded people.

The people closest to you have the greatest impact on your life. Surrounding yourself with people who drag you down will have a detrimental impact on you. I know it certainly did on me.

Your inner circle should be your cheerleaders: they need to be strong and positive. It can be made up of friends, family, trusted advisors, mentors, spiritual leaders or spouses. Importantly, the relationship you have with those in your inner circle should be based on trust, honesty and respect: anything less and they will not contribute to your wellbeing. Your inner circle needs to be people who will call to the best in you and be willing to challenge you on your choices, if those choices do not serve you well.

There is a great proverb which says: "Become wise by walking with the wise; hang out with fools and watch your life fall to pieces."

I am not saying you need to change everyone in your inner circle all at once, but I am saying you will need to know who is adding value to you, and who is not, as you take this journey within to discover **Remarkable You**!

Focus Points:

- Who is currently in your inner circle?
- What influence does your inner circle have on you?
- Does your inner circle mostly lift you up or drag you down?

Action Steps for Your Journey:

- If your inner circle is not the right influence on you, make a decision to consciously subtract from and add to your inner circle. Make your choice based on who is influential in calling to the best in you and leads by example. If these people are missing, start to look at who could play that role for you. Make a list in your journal.
- Consider how you add value to those in your inner circle. The best relationships are reciprocal: are you holding up your end? Are there people who take from you without giving in return?

Chapter 13

The Dangers of Hidden Baggage

During those nine years as a teacher aide, I built within myself a real confidence in, and respect for, this 'New Wendy'. I had changed my attitude from hopeless to hopeful, and that helped me to behave differently. I stepped out of my comfort zone and discovered I was capable of far more than I ever imagined. I found this hidden potential buried under my baggage.

If you are reading this and feeling down-hearted about the idea it might take you a decade to find the remarkable in you, please do not. Everyone's journey is different, and part of the reason mine took so long is I figured all this stuff out for myself through trial and error. Just the fact you are reading this book puts you ahead of me!

Although the period at the school and the support of my cheer squad helped me create a 'New Wendy', I had not reconciled with 'Old Wendy'. I still carried my baggage, because I had not dealt with it. I thought it did not matter, because it was hidden in the deep, dark recesses of my heart and mind where it could only reveal itself in my thoughts to me.

The 'Old Wendy' was still covered in shame. I did not

want anyone who knew 'New Wendy' to see that. I certainly did not share anything about my past, or the dark thoughts that still haunted me. I was about to discover that even hidden baggage is dangerous.

Even though I was making changes in my life, and my life was much different to that of my parents, the shame that attached itself to me in childhood was still dragging me down. Even in a growth period and in a supportive environment, all the *bogus stories* I had collected about myself in the past were still infecting my outlook.

In chapter 1 I talked about what happened at school, how other children and teachers told me I was dirty, different, no good. Those words attached themselves to me and became my identity. As a child I often pretended to be someone different because I had learned I was 'not enough'. In many ways I was still pretending to be someone different. Although from the outside it looked like I was succeeding, on the inside I struggled, always thinking I could never measure up.

Now I see it is like this: we attach labels and judgments to ourselves like stickers, one on top of the other. I started to collect mine as a child and continued to collect them well into my adulthood. My baggage was full and heavy, and decorated with the labels other people had placed on me.

Believing that 'myself' was not worthy of belonging, I coped by copying the image of the people I wanted to emulate. I dressed like the women I worked with at the school, and I learned to speak like them. It is great to have examples of how to dress and speak and behave, but we are meant to be the very best version of ourselves, not a copy of someone else. I did not know that then.

Have you heard of impostor syndrome? It is the feeling we are a fraud, no matter how prepared we are, or experienced at what we do, and any minute now someone will find us out and expose us. Everyone suffers from impostor syndrome at some stage in their life, but when you have created a false facade to trick everyone into believing you belong, the feeling you are a fraud can be overwhelming. You 'know for certain' you do not really belong.

Being offered the job in government seemed like a real victory. I did not realize I was pinning my self-worth on superficial external things. 'New Wendy', who talked differently and dressed differently won that job, not the hidden, shameful 'Real Wendy'. 'Real Wendy' was only mine to know about, I had to hide her from others, because 'Real Wendy' would not be acceptable.

What happened next added to my shame.

The manager who was supposed to be my immediate boss in the new job had been on the panel that interviewed and appointed me, but the wheels of government turned slowly, and by the time I was due to start the role, the manager had changed.

The new manager invited me to meet with her before I started, so she could get to know me. Let me set the scene: We met in her office in the Brisbane. I was dressed for the part, looking very professional and capable, but inside I was nervous about stepping out of the safety of the school, where I was surrounded by women who believed in me and saw potential in me that I still did not see. Moving away from that environment into a very big unknown was a giant step for me, and I felt the enormity of it as I sat down at that meeting. Then my new boss said to me, "You would not have been my choice for this role, I would have appointed someone else."

Shame flooded over me. All I could think in that moment was she saw right through me. Past my professional look, past the smile on my face to the 'Real Wendy', the dirty, different one who was not capable, and certainly not worthy of this role. That was it, I was not good enough! I would not have been her choice! I did not measure up to the required standard!

That woman confirmed all the thoughts and feelings I hid from the world. All my hard work, and she saw through it all! My fear this newly invented Wendy was not enough, that I would never be enough, had come true.

Walking away from that meeting, my baggage was heavier than ever with her judgments weighing it down. How could I be what she wanted? I had already left the job at the school, what was I to do now? What mask could I wear to prove she was wrong, that I was capable? Even as I asked myself the question, my fears spoke: "*You are not capable. Walk away.*" The old, hopeless tapes started playing: "*This is way too hard. I cannot do this, I cannot go on. Here we go again, not good enough.*"

The old pattern was there, you know: when it all gets too hard, I can always take my parents' way out. I felt sick with the anticipated shame of telling my husband and letting him down.

But then that little seed of hope, that by then I had grown into a sapling strong enough to resist the wintry wind of her judgment, reminded me it was there. It told me not to run, but to hang on and fight. I got angry, and I decided to prove her wrong.

To run would mean to fail and I did not want to fail. I decided it must be different this time, I must *be* different. I did not know where that impulse came from, but it grew into a deep determination to show that manager her judgment of me was wrong.

There are people in our lives for a season and reason. The teachers from that school had seen something in me, and so did my husband Bill, who could now see a capability in me that had not been there earlier in our married life. There are times in our lives when we need to borrow the belief of others, others who believe in you and ride the waves of that belief until you build our own. That is what I did!

There is a great quote from poet Frederick Langbridge: "Two men looked out through prison bars; one saw mud, the other saw the stars." Both men were in identical circumstances, but their perspectives were entirely different. One looked for beauty and found it; the other focused on ugliness and found it.

It works like this: our circumstances in life produce certain emotions. So how do you change your emotional response when you feel powerless over people and circumstances? By changing how you think about them! True change always begins in your mind.

That manager and I went on to become great friends and we still are today.

Reflection: Dealing with Hidden Baggage

"Thoughts lead on to purpose, purpose leads on to actions, actions form habits, habits decide character, and character fixes our destiny."
Tyron Edwards

We all have them, moments of flight or fight. Run from the circumstance, the words, the comments, the *bogus stories* … or stay and fight for what we believe. A defining moment when we get to make a choice about how we respond, and in that moment we show our true character. Those moments can be as brief as seconds, but feel like hours.

What we think, how we react, and what action we take in those situations becomes pivotal to our future and the baggage we are carrying will affect the choices we make in those moments. So it is important we deal with our hidden baggage.

Let me say again: no matter what you have done, you are not beyond hope. But if you cannot be honest about who you really are, the fear of exposure will always hold you back from pursuing your true potential.

Sow a thought, reap an action.
Sow an action, reap a habit.
Sow a habit, reap a character.
Sow a character, reap a destiny.

Focus Points:

- Do you have hidden baggage? Are there aspects of your story you hide out of shame?
- When faced with a challenge or a *bogus story* moment, do you respond by fleeing the circumstance or standing for what you believe is your truth?
- Has your baggage affected what you do in those moments?

Action Steps for Your Journey:

It is time **Remarkable You** … to empty out that hidden baggage! What action can you take to turn that baggage upside down and get rid of the rubbish once and for all? Use **ACT** to develop a plan in your journal.

It might not be easy. You might need professional help. It will not happen all at once. If you have experienced trauma, it can take years to heal. Each time you shake free a piece of that baggage your heart will be lighter, and you will hold your head higher, and you will be ready to refill your bag with the treasures you collect as you travel to your future!

It is time to **ACT**

A – decide what **action** you will take
C – identify what **choices** you will make
T – commit to a **time-frame** for this change

Chapter 14

Growing Self-worth

I took the borrowed belief of my inner circle into that new role, along with my changed mindset and the skills I knew I had developed. After my time at the school I was confident in my ability to encourage and equip others with my words and actions and proud of my newly developed ability to build relationships and give leadership. Armed with those weapons I set about proving that manager wrong!

It was not easy in the beginning, but as time passed I started to build a reputation of being someone who cared and would listen. This became part of my area of expertise. What I did was treat people the way I wanted to be treated. I became the go-to person for fixing difficult workplaces where there were complaints and bullying that affected the individual staff and the business.

I wonder if you are thinking right now, how could this be possible? In hindsight, it seems to me this was all part of the plan for my life, as unbelievable as that may seem to others. What it taught me was that when we set our mind to do something (for the right or wrong reasons!) and stick to that decision no matter what, you will succeed. I set out to prove I was worthy of my role, and that is what I did.

Little did I realize that was I was pinning my self-worth to that job title and not to my true, remarkable self.

I worked in that role for three years, bringing about transformational, restorative change to people and their workplaces. I built such a reputation for integrity, actions and outcomes that I received a Queensland Public Service Australia Day award for my work. This reinforced in my mind that the position, and the title that came with it, proved my worth.

How confused was my thinking? Our job title is just that: a title, another label. It does not in any way make us who we are. Who we are; the values we believe; the character traits we have; the behaviors we exhibit … those are all things we bring to a position. The label does not make us, we make the label have meaning.

My title became my mask, and it made me feel worthy. We all have times in our lives when we wear a mask to hide who we really are. In my case, I still had not dealt with my shame about my childhood, my anger towards those who harmed me or the insidious temptation of suicide that was still trying to seduce me. These things were still in my thoughts and deep recesses of my heart just waiting for me, waiting behind the mask for the right moment to get my attention again.

After three years in that role, I applied for and was appointed to a senior leadership role in the same department where I was to lead a multi-disciplinary team of prosecutors for the State Government. Knowing where I had come from this seemed like a miracle.

This new role was to lead to the next big step on my journey to discovering the remarkable within me, but not in the way you might think.

In the role, I led and managed matters that went before the courts. The team had been quite dysfunctional and hence my reputation for sorting out difficult workplaces helped me secure the role. My first job in government was a steep learning curve: this new job was even steeper climb. I had no idea of the business, but I had learned a lot about people and how to equip and lead them. I ended up being in the role for seven years and I became very much attached to the title and the status it gave me. Sure, I worked hard and delivered good results, but this story is not about the job.

This story is about how I discovered the remarkable within me, and even with all my achievements, after all that time, I still did not believe I was remarkable. I still did not have that intrinsic self-worth and, as you will soon see, I learned the hard way the external symbols of success are a flimsy gilt facade, and the real gold has to be found within.

Reflection: Self-worth

I stopped believing some of the *bogus stories* other people told me as a child and believed myself more worthy as a result of my career success, but sadly my self-worth was now attached to my job. I was still seeking approval from outside of me. I had developed some self-esteem but I had not learned the lesson about self-worth.

Although self-worth is often used as a synonym for self-esteem, psychologist Dr. Lisa Firestone says "self-worth should be less about measuring yourself based on external actions and more about valuing your inherent worth as a person." In other words, self-worth is about who you are, not about what you do.

Dr Robert Firestone, her father, developed the concept of the 'anti-self': the enemy within that speaks to us with a critical voice. It is like a cruel coach inside our heads telling us we are worthless or undeserving of happiness—but it is coming from us! This 'anti-self' is shaped from painful childhood experiences, critical attitudes we were exposed to early in life, and the feelings our parents had about themselves. Over time, these attitudes have become so ingrained in us that as adults we do not even recognize the voice as the enemy, instead accepting their destructive point of view as our own. That was exactly my experience.

A high degree of self-worth naturally enhances our self-esteem, thereby providing us with the self-confidence we need to follow through with our decisions about choices and actions.

Focus Points:

- Do you see your intrinsic worth as a person or have you allowed your critical inner voice to coach you into believing you are unworthy?
- Do you think how you are is fixed, and can never change, or do you believe you can grow and change?

Action Steps for Your Journey:

- As you start to build a greater awareness of self-worth, knowing your self-worth is about who you are and not what you do, can you notice when you criticize yourself?
- Practice thinking about yourself in different ways. Rephrasing your words and thoughts will make a powerful difference: For example, change "I am scared and worthless" to "I am courageous and capable." We can define our lives by what we think.
- Use hopeful statements to describe situations. For example, "no matter what happens, this is just a moment and I will get through this because there is better ahead."
- Treat yourself with kindness: remember sow a thought, reap an action.

Chapter 15

Fighting for Your Remarkable Self

I enjoyed my leadership role in government, and I became very attached to the status it gave me. I thought I had conquered my fears, and buried 'Old Wendy', but really I had built a facade out of external symbols of success. I looked the part, I had the job title and the big office in the city, and I thought that meant I had fulfilled my childhood vision. Then one day everything that made me feel worthy was abruptly taken away from me.

On 21 September 2009, I was asked to attend a meeting with my General Manager, a woman who had recently been appointed to the role. She was ex-military, had a very strong personality and very intimidating to me. She did not know much about me at all and certainly did not know my integrity. At that meeting, she told me I was being investigated by the Crime and Misconduct Commission (CMC). The CMC investigate very serious complaints against government officials.

I went numb. I could still hear the General Manager's voice, but the emotional impact was overwhelming. I was informed I could not be told who complained, or what the allegations against me were, except one was blackmail of a government official. I was told not to talk to my staff, or tell anyone about the complaint except for my family and a support person. I was stood down from my role, and removed immediately from my workplace—marched out of the building like a criminal.

Everything I thought I was, snatched away in one brief meeting. All those things still hidden in the darkest recesses of my heart—the shame of my childhood and insidious spirit of suicide that was still trying to run me down—came flooding in, washing away all my imagined purpose and value.

Shame is humiliation, mortification, discredit, dishonor and disgrace and I was filled with them all. My hidden baggage, waiting in the wings all this time, suddenly stepped up to center stage ready to take over and it demanded top billing! All the things I felt made me important and worthy disappeared instantly in an avalanche of shame and disgrace. Deep inside I knew I had done nothing wrong in my role because integrity was always at the forefront of every action I took, but in that moment it did not matter.

When the approval of others is paramount for your self-worth, when you pin your hopes and desires on other people's opinions, or external things like a title or possessions that you believe make you worthy, it is *bogus stories* you are believing. Those *bogus stories* are a flimsy facade, no replacement for the solid foundation of self-worth. And when shame is also in the equation, remember shame is one of the biggest *bogus stories* there is. And there I was, smack bang in the midst of that scenario. I was so filled with shame I could not even tell my husband right away.

I could not drive, I was so emotionally distressed, so the General Manager had someone from Human Resources Department drive me. Instead of going to Bill, I went to a friend, who I will call Jean. The appearance of things was so important in my life then, and I attached myself to Jean because in my mind she was everything I was not, and everything I wanted to be. In my mind she was perfect and had the perfect family, things which were way out of my reach, or so I thought. I attached myself to Jean in an unhealthy friendship because I wanted to be like, look like and be accepted by her. I went to Jean's house because, right then and there, her opinion mattered to me and I did not want to call my husband. I spent many hours with this lady, seeking her approval, asking her to sanction that I was okay.

I was so filled with disgrace, I did not even tell my husband Bill. I went home at my normal finish time. Deep inside I did not want to tell him because of the shame of it all, but also because I had failed him. Somehow I found the words, and the dear man responded with so much grace and kindness towards me. My guilt was never an issue for him, he knew my integrity, he was just angry at the anonymous perpetrators who had instigated this action against me.

The next 24 hours changed my life.

Shame, guilt and thoughts of suicide had been

hounding me since my dad's death. Up until then, I had been able fight them off, but my experience had taught me, when the pain gets too much, the answer is to take your life. That is what my parents had instilled in me. It was hidden inside me just waiting to take over at the right time, and the time was now! This new humiliation was the most overwhelming pain. The foundations of everything I thought I had built seemed to be crumbling around me. The answer seemed obvious.

I did not sleep that night, the pain of loss was too great. I had lost my identity, all I believed I was; my title, my position, as far as I was concerned all my worth was gone. It was all gone and it had been replaced with shame! Losing all this, meant I lost who I was. My mind was working overtime replaying those old tapes, those old destructive thought patterns over and over.

The next morning, the city where I lived, Brisbane, was hit by one of the biggest red dust storms in its history. It was all over Australia: so bad that it is reported in Wikipedia. It made the sky turn dark, much like my heart and soul that morning. My husband went off to work as usual, having no idea of what was happening in my mind. Why would he? I never shared my deep hidden thoughts. That is what shame does, it does not allow you to tell anyone.

By now I was part of a church community, still trying to find out more about this God who told me I had not killed my dad. I was a 'Christian' who often contemplated suicide so how on earth could I tell anyone in this church community? I could not measure up, even in church, even as a Christian, that is what I thought.

After Bill left for work, I sat on my lounge for many hours playing my options over and over in my mind, looking for any possible way forward, but there was none. Everything was lost, how could I face this?

It was never about the allegations—at that stage I did not even know what they all were. It was about the loss. It was about what others would think, what would happen to my job. I knew, if nothing else, I had integrity and I was sure my decision-making processes were professional, but in the scheme of things to me that morning, those things did not matter.

What was happening seemed beyond comprehension. The pain of loss, loss of my worth and identity, who I perceived I was, overtook any practical sense of all this mess. Death was teasing me, telling me if I chose him the pain would be gone, and my family could get on with their lives. The darkness of the dust storm closed in on the darkness of my soul and the insidious thing that chased me for so long finally had me in its grip. My car was in the garage, I could use that to finish my life once and for all.

In moments like these any sense of clarity is gone. Any sense this is not okay does not exist. You are only looking for a way to ease the pain. I knew I had options, my parents had shown me that. I had carried this knowledge for the past 42 years, now it was my turn. I remember very clearly laying on the floor in a fetal position, sobbing as all the anger, guilt, unforgiveness and shame flooded over me. I lost all track of time and in the midst of it all, I remembered something my dad told me.

He told me there was such a darkness over him, it would battle with him for his life, but I was 13 and this meant nothing to me, it was just my dad in one of his moods. But as the incredible darkness tempted me to the ultimate escape, I remembered and understood, and that triggered a desire deep within me to fight back. I could see Bill's face and the faces of my children and I remembered how I felt when I witnessed my dad die. I remembered all the horror and the pain that still hounded me.

My choices were becoming clearer. I had two choices, fight this or give in, fight *hard*, do *whatever it takes*, or give up and accept my parents' destiny as my own. The choice was mine!

I was fighting the battle my parents had fought and lost: they were not strong enough and the darkness succeeded and took their lives.

Would I be strong enough?

Reflection: Defining moments

A *defining moment* is a point in your life when you are urged to make a pivotal decision, or when you experience something which fundamentally changes you. Not only do these moments define us, but they have a transformative effect on our perceptions and behaviors.

Defining moments, we will all have them … maybe not all as dramatic as this one; or maybe even worse. Some may be life and death decisions … some may not … but each one is like standing at a crossroad and deciding which way to go.

The choice we make in that moment will define our future. Not only will what we do in these moments have a life impact on us, it will also impact on those around us. The choices we make and the actions we take may have generational impacts—just like my parents' choices impacted on me.

Maybe in the past when these defining moments have come along, you have made choices that did not serve your potential, just as I did. Remember, it is never too late to start making better choices.

The most important point in this, is know there is always a way forward, always a choice, a choice for life itself and always hope for the future. To quote Helen Keller, "Hope sees the invisible, feels the intangible and achieves the impossible."

If you cannot find it on your own you *must* seek

help to find your hope. Hopelessness is a kind of hell on earth, and that is why it so often leads to the belief that suicide is a way out.

Focus Points:

- What have been the defining moments in your story so far?
- With what you have learned, with hindsight, do you see different choices you could have made that would have created a different path forward?

Action Steps for Your Journey:

- As you read this book, perhaps this is a defining moment for you, maybe you are right now, standing at a crossroad not sure which way to go—if that is where you find yourself take the time to consider your actions going forward.
- What choice can you make right now, in this moment in time, that will set you on this new path of *hope*?
- Write it out and hold yourself accountable for your choice. Remember, even a 1% change for the better will bring exponential change. You can do this—remember **You Are Remarkable!**

Chapter 16

A True Battle Moment

What I am about to share may seem unbelievable to some readers, but it is my truth. There is no point telling my story unless I share what really happened.

Back to 22 September 2009, to the struggle for my life; the physical and mental battle over whether to give up on life or to fight. It is as clear as if it was yesterday.

Sobbing, wracked with misery on my lounge room floor, I battled the overwhelming darkness that promised me a false peace. I fought the desire to die, the desire to kill the pain, to no longer have this battle, to finally go the way of my dad and mum. As I fought that enemy within, that malevolent thing that so wanted me to go down the same road as my parents, I remember clearly crying out to God, to Jesus and reaching out my hand. Without even realizing it, by putting my hand out, in an instinctive desire to touch something, I was stepping out in faith, in the faith that God would move in … and He did! It was instantaneous!

> *"You will seek me and find me when you seek me with all of your heart."*
> **Jeremiah 29:13**

Whatever the darkness was, wherever it had come from, it dispelled in that moment. I lay there on the floor trying to comprehend what had just happened? The darkness I felt was gone! In its place was a quiet, a calm; I felt I could catch my breath, it was so serene. You may not share my Christian beliefs but I ask you to believe me when I say that moment in my lounge room set me free from the power of my past and onto a path to discover the remarkable within me.

My circumstances did not change in an instant, that is not how life works *but* whatever it was that made me want to give in, gave up. I knew my truth. I knew I had done nothing wrong and I deserved justice, and I was prepared to stand up for myself. I had found my self-worth.

I still had to endure the investigation, stand up to the perceived shame that was attached to them and face down my accusers, but the desire to end my life finished that day with my decision to fight.

That insidious suicidal inheritance which had been passed down through the generations would stop with me. It no longer had power over me nor would I pass it to the generations to come behind me. Hand on my heart, I can honestly say, it has never come back. It was no longer there in the deep parts of my heart waiting to overtake me and run me down. The shame of being marched out of that government building in front of all my staff and the anger at being falsely accused … all of it was still there, but it was no longer attached to suicide.

I was given some days off work to process what had happened and then placed in an office which housed government executives for the duration of the investigation. I was not given any work to do. The office I was given was on display for all to see and the rumor mill was running rampant with all sorts of gossip.

I believe management would have preferred I left, so the department would not have to undergo the investigation, a much easier, time and money saving option for them, but my integrity was important to me. I was not prepared to walk away after everything I had been through. I won the initial battle for my life, so the investigation would be easier … or so I thought.

As we know a journey always begins with the first step, but how could I face going to work every day with all those people judging me? Other people's opinions were of utmost importance to me then, but how could I get through it, with all the words spoken, the lies and innuendo all around me? Let me tell you what I did.

Come back with me to my lounge room, where the battle that changed my life took place. As I sat on my floor and cried out to Jesus, other burdens were broken off me.

There was such a realization, even if I did not understand it, that somewhere, somehow to this God, to this Jesus, I mattered! I mattered enough for that lady to tell me God knew my father's death was not my fault. I mattered enough that when I reached out in faith to

Jesus, I was saved from sure death. And if I mattered, then who I was, must have been okay at some level, in some way.

I realized I had carried the anger in my baggage for way too long, and it no longer served me well. I realized I was carrying so much unforgiveness in my heart.

Unforgiveness towards my dad for placing me in that position, asking me to hand him the gun.

Unforgiveness towards my Uncle Ted for taking advantage of my innocence in the most horrific moments of my life.

Unforgiveness towards my mum for exposing me to my uncle; not being able to protect me, my sisters and brother as children; and for expecting me to take responsibility for her.

And, hardest of all, unforgiveness towards myself for all my perceived failures.

I had seen this unforgiveness play out in my life with its nasty little friend; the shame I held deep in the crevices of my heart as bitterness and resentment. Little did I realize, as I went through the process of forgiving, the person I would be releasing was going to be myself.

Up until then, I always saw forgiving people who hurt me as being hard. It seemed so unfair for them to receive forgiveness when I had been hurt. I got pain and they got their freedom, released from what they had done without having to pay for the pain they caused. Now I realize it was me who I was releasing.

The forgiveness did not come right away, on the floor of my living room. But the desire to let go of the anger, for my sake, did. Just like any journey to discovering something new, it takes time and it requires searching and uncovering. If I was going to do that step by step, I wanted to know more.

Up until then my understanding of church, the Bible and God was limited. My participation was always about wanting approval, so I would just jump onto the coat tail of what someone else believed. I decided this was my time to understand and so I used my time in forced exile in that sterile government office to find out who I was and why I mattered, and to learn how to forgive those who had hurt me.

The timing of this was so significant, as it ultimately allowed me to forgive those who had made the false allegations to the CMC. Oh my goodness, what a relief that was for me. I felt so much lighter in my heart. Sure, I still had to work through this daily, and there were many times I had to remind myself I had forgiven these people and would not allow that poison to seep back into my heart and life, but I practiced what I had learned and it got easier as time passed. What a journey!

Every time we encounter a painful experience, we get to know ourselves a little better. Until now, all I had done was allow pain to diminish me, but not anymore. I was ready to face the pain, and I grew to such a greater level of awareness of myself. Facing the pain forced me to face who I was and literally discover the true me. Not 'New Wendy' or 'Old Wendy', just Wendy: all of me, good and bad. As I looked in the mirror I saw Wendy, no longer with the shadow darkness of the 'Old Wendy' but the beauty of what could be.

When life becomes difficult, when cracks spread through our existence and our strength seems to leak out, fill the gaps with hope. Like gold adorning distressed antique art, hope will reinforce, add value, and reveal more beauty …

Reflection: Forgiveness

> "To forgive is to set a prisoner free and discover that the prisoner was you."
> Lewis B. Smedes

When you hold onto pain and resentment you suffer because the sorrow is intensified to keep it alive. To withhold forgiveness keeps alive emotions of suffering, hurt, anger and blame which discolor your perception of life … but only in you. The person who caused you harm is not affected by your pain in the slightest.

Forgiveness does not mean forgetting. Its motive is preserved in self-forgiveness and the role you may have played in co-creating the circumstances, such as when I handed my father the gun. This does not mean I consented to what transpired. Given your involvement, even as a victim, you forgive yourself regardless of your role. Forgiveness means to let go of hatred, instead of allowing it to eat at you.

Author Dennis Merritt Jones put it this way:

> *"At the end of the day, forgiveness is really not for the other person's benefit at all—it's for our own. Regardless of how illogical it may seem at times, it is through unconditional forgiveness that we surrender the past to the past and enter the present, freeing ourselves to stand in the infinite Light that knows how to heal our deepest and most painful wounds."*

To forgive, avoid reflecting on thoughts of being victimized. Do not play the tapes that churn up those old emotions. Trust the power of forgiveness to heal the hurt and pain *for you*. It might take some time, and you might have to keep reminding yourself you have forgiven when those thought patterns come back to you, but one day you will notice you have been released from the prison of past pain.

As Nelson Mandala avowed to the African National Congress, "Forgiveness starts here. Forgiveness liberates the soul, it removes fear, that is why it is such a powerful weapon. The past is the past, we look to the future."

You cannot look forward to the future when you are forever turning your head to look back to the past. Forgiveness puts the past behind you.

Focus Points:

- Have you been holding onto unforgiveness?
- How does the unforgiveness affect you emotionally?
- Can you see where this unforgiveness is getting in your way of moving forward?

Action Steps for Your Journey:

- Use your journal to record all the areas in your life where you need to unconditionally forgive yourself.
- Take the time to forgive yourself for each one: write it down, and say it aloud. This might be emotional, so give yourself space for that. It might feel fake at first: keep practicing.
- Specifically identify who else you need to forgive and for what reason you need to forgive them. Write it in your journal.
- Take the time to unconditionally forgive each of those who have harmed you. Forgiveness does not mean you need to bring these people into your inner circle, but it does mean releasing yourself. This might just mean writing it in your journal: you do not have to have a confrontation with the person.
- You can use words like "I choose not to blame or hold the actions of (name) against him/her. Where I have felt betrayed by (name), I forgive them."

Chapter 17

Remarkable Me

The nine months of the investigation became an opportunity to experience personal growth. Every day I had to go to an office, where I had no work to do. I had to run the gauntlet of stares and gossip. I made a choice to respond with dignity. Because I had already been working so hard to understand the effect of my attitude on myself and others, I knew my attitude would play a big role. So, I did not hide or act guilty. I held my head high, fortified with a prayer written on paper and tucked in my bra. I did not let on that I felt shame and humiliation.

As I said earlier, I cannot tell my story and skip this chapter about how I found a relationship with God. I am not pressing you to believe what I believe, all I am asking is that you read this story and see how this played out in my life. We are all different, and we each find our own way. Your journey may not involve God, or at least not a Christian idea of God, but my experience working with clients has taught me that to unshackle the remarkable within, we all need to explore faith.

I had so much time as I sat in that office to reflect on

who I was, and who this God was. Was He someone I could trust? Who was Jesus? Why did I matter to them enough for them to rescue me? Why did I consider I was not good enough? Why had other people's opinions always been at the forefront of my mind? It was perfect timing in so many ways.

All the opinions and comments made to me, and about me, in those nine months gave me fodder for discovery. They provoked a deeper awareness of my responses and how I had been sabotaging myself.

Sure, I still had this investigation going on in the background, but as I said, I knew I had done nothing wrong, and I had no thought in my mind I would be found guilty. All I needed was to take this journey no matter how hard it was and to learn the power of *resilience*. Maybe this was simple blind faith, but that is what I held onto and it became my pillar of strength to get me through.

Our belief drives behavior and this belief helped drive mine. I learned a whole new meaning of trust: in who I knew I was, and in this new idea of God. I found myself learning more about myself every day, who I was and who I was meant to be. I was taking responsibility for myself, my actions and my thoughts in a whole new way.

This was an uphill journey, but I learned through this time that everything worthwhile is uphill! All growth requires some struggle: and it all takes time. If you are dedicated to revealing the remarkable within you then you must be committed to handling bad experiences. The greater the struggle, the more triumphant the outcome.

Over these months I took time to find out who God was

for me and why I mattered to Him. I started to see I was created for a purpose, I had a destiny, not my mother's, not my father's, not someone else's that I wanted to copy, but my very own destiny, that I had a free will to design. This was such a mind shift from feeling totally unworthy, to having a strong sense of purpose and value.

I put my faith in a Heavenly Father who loved and cared for me and wanted a relationship with me. This was such a new and great concept. (I have shared more on this in the epilogue). Remember I talked about our fundamental need for belonging? I discovered through having faith each one of us was created in love and, to be part of a greater purpose helps us understand we all belong because we are all part of creation. We do not have to prove ourselves to anyone.

I have also talked about how our choices have an impact on us. In the midst of that awful time, I was still able to make choices that served the remarkable in me. My choice to stay and fight, and hold onto my truth during the investigation, had an unexpected impact: those watching me closely in that workplace, and in my family, saw this new, transformed Wendy. They saw how I handled myself, my attitude and behavior. Remember the vision I had when I was sixteen, that I would become a woman of influence? Well, it was coming true before my very eyes. I carried so much influence in that time, not because of my title, not because of my work, but because of the choices I made.

I found out that women of influence—influential leaders—do not step down from their values and integrity. Influential leaders stay the course. Once you choose a course of action, it is just a matter of walking it out daily. I found out I was an influential leader. I learned that people watch leaders when things do not go according to plan: in the good, the bad and sometimes ugly moments of our lives. It is the 'Law of The Picture' as my mentor and coach John C Maxwell would say, "*It is what people see.*"

Let me tell you right now, everyone is a leader and it starts with leading ourselves well. We never know how the influence we carry will look and feel to those around us. I believe the influence we carry is beyond measure. Just like I watched my parents and saw what they did, so many were watching me. No matter how difficult it was on some days, I never deviated from my course.

My new-found trust and faith grew more and more every day.

It was seven months before I found out the nature of all the allegations made against me—approximately 300 altogether. I had made enemies in that senior leadership role by doing my job and holding people accountable for their actions in the workplace. When I finally had an opportunity to read all the allegations, this new-found true Wendy, *remarkable* Wendy, could laugh at them. It was the laugh of faith. Some people do not like to be held accountable, and that was the trigger for the false allegation.

One day as I sat in the office journaling, waiting to find out the allegations and outcome, I felt God tell me He would lay a table before me amid my enemies. What on earth could that mean? Well, look what happened next:

Nine months to the date after I was removed from the workplace, all the allegations were found to be false! After

I was cleared of the allegations, the department put on a morning tea to announce my innocence and a public apology was made in front of my enemies, including those I supervised and held accountable. Nothing like it had ever happened before. I faced those people, knowing I stood in my truth, and proved myself. For the first time in my life, I believed I was remarkable. With this new-found understanding, I changed my whole outlook.

That day it seemed as though my long ago vision had come true but in the years that have passed since, my influence has continued to grow. I no longer put a limit on what that vision might mean.

After I was cleared of the allegations, I went into another senior leadership role managing the major contracts for the State Government. This time my worth was not about the title, but who I was to the core; the values I lived and the skill base I had to contribute, including my integrity, tested in fire.

My integrity, attitude and behavior had been witnessed by the executive of the department that I was placed in throughout the investigation. When I left, some two years later to start my own consultancy, I was engaged to come back as a consultant to teach on integrity and attitude.

I found out who I really was through this chapter of my story. What was meant to diminish me ended up having the opposite effect and instead it worked as a catalyst of growth. I found out who I was actually created to be, not someone else's version of me, not a title, not a position that said who I was, but the true version of Wendy Burns!

Reflection: Faith

I survived this trial-by-fire; this journey of overcoming suicide, dealing with shame, learning about forgiveness, and finding out I mattered by putting my new-found faith in God between me and the circumstances I faced. My circumstances did not change, but how I saw myself and my circumstances did change.

All the way through this book I have spoken to you about the importance of making your own choices and taking responsibility for your own life. This chapter is no different. I value each person who has taken the time to read this book. Each and every one of you are remarkable! I am not asking you to believe my faith, but I know you need to find your faith.

Remember, I said **HOPE** is **H**anging **O**n in **P**atient **E**xpectation? Well, I see **FAITH** as

Future
Answers
In
The
Hope

Hope is the belief we can aspire to reach our true and full potential. **Faith** is the belief we are connected to something bigger than ourselves, a loving force that wants us to achieve the potential we were created with. Working with coaching clients over many years, I have found these definitions work regardless of the individual's religious belief.

This faith of mine was birthed out of my desperate struggle that awful day, and strengthened through those long hard months where I was forced to walk among my enemies and sit alone in a sterile office five days a week. Those months allowed me to determine who this God was for me and who I was in Him. That faith allowed my story to continue and stopped me giving in to hopelessness, shame and guilt. I discovered I had a true purpose for my life, way beyond what I could perceive.

Faith may mean something different to you, but trust me when I say there is always a bigger picture. Sometimes we will see it and sometimes we may never know, but by trusting in that bigger picture, we gain perspective on our struggles and find the energy to fortify us as we create our future.

Focus Points:

- What does faith mean to you?
- Do you feel a connection to something bigger than you?
- In the past, where have you put your faith?

Action Steps for Your Journey:

- Where do you need to add faith to your story?
- Write in your journal about the areas of your life that need more faith. Where can you draw faith from? What stories do you have about faith from your past? Are they good stories, or *bogus stories*?

Future
Answers
In
The
Hope

Chapter 18

Remarkable YOU

Every one of us is remarkable.
YOU ARE REMARKABLE.

I told you these things right at the beginning. I hope by this point, you are at least starting to believe me. The gold within us is so often hidden, buried beneath the dirt and the grime we have been exposed to, or covered ourselves in: we rarely see the glint of gold shining from within unless we are looking for it.

This journey is one of self-discovery, where you dig deep to find out who you really are. It will not always be easy, and it will take time, but you can start today. I promise if you take one step, and then another, before long you will have journeyed far, and you will find the scenery is quite different.

You *will* discover the
Remarkable You.

In marathons in ancient Greece, a torch was handed to each runner at the starting line. To win, a runner had to cross the finish line with their torch still burning. The torch race was a tough one which led through mountains and valleys. Doubtless there were times when others would pass the winning runner by, when their strength would fail, when they lost their way or stumbled, when they had to retrace their steps to get back on track. But what counted in this race was not the style, but the staying power.

> *"For everyone to whom much is given, much is required."*
> **Luke 12:48**

We are each called to run our best race and to cross the finish line with the torch in our hearts till burning. I know I will finish this race well, with my torch still burning. How do I know? Because I now know who I am. I am a remarkable woman: a woman of influence, a woman of faith. I know it is important to me to:

- care about and value people
- make a difference in all I do
- add value to those I meet, no matter who they are or what circumstances they are in
- always continue to grow until the day I die
- lead by example through the good, bad and ugly: no matter what.

I know I get to decide each and every day how I will write my story:

- I will be intentional about how I write it.
- I will allow the passion that burns in my heart for helping others to guide my actions.
- I will help others to discover their passion, to know their dream matters, their purpose matters, *they* matter.

I know in all this, my attitude will color everything I do. I have learned to be quick to forgive and seek forgiveness when I get it wrong, and I know I will slip up, and I will struggle but I will extend myself the same compassion and kindness I extend others.

You are no less remarkable than me. You can, and should, feel like your life matters. *You matter*. You owe it to yourself to unshackle the remarkable within you, to reveal your hidden vein of gold and enable it to shine. If you have not already started taking the steps outlined in each chapter, I encourage you to do so now. If you need to, borrow my belief in you, and step forward.

Let's review the steps

1. Let go of shame—do not let the ultimate *bogus story* be your truth. You are worthy, no matter what.

2. Take responsibility for you—do not try to control others, or take responsibility for their actions, and do not let others control you.

3. Reject false friends—self-worth has to come from within, do not seek others' approval, especially if doing so exposes you to harm.

4. Acknowledge the pain—recognize the ways you numb, and distract yourself.

5. Reject hopelessness—hopelessness will lead you on a downward spiral, that can only end in tragedy.

6. Discover hope—it is always there, even though the seed may be small. Keep searching until you find it! **H**ang **O**n with **P**atient **E**xpectation that you can achieve your full potential.

7. Beware bogus stories—especially the ones you tell yourself. Be mindful of the words you use. The words we speak about ourselves have power.

8. Empower hope—give water and sunshine to that little seed of hope so it can sustain you on the uphill journey of growth.

9. Become a futurist—your history is not your destiny, unless you choose to give it that power. You cannot affect the past but you sure can affect the future ... by making choices that serve your aspirations.

10. Manage your attitude—your attitude is one thing you can always control, and it will be the difference maker in all sorts of situations.

11. Be accountable to *you*—your trust and belief in yourself will grow as you make commitments to yourself, and stick to them.

12. Choose your inner circle—surround yourself with people who help build you up, not the ones who would drag you down.

13. Clear out your hidden baggage—release yourself from the shackles on your potential by facing your darkest secrets and fears.

14. Grow your self-worth—silence that critical inner coach and focus on living your values rather than pursuing external symbols of success.

15. Build strength for a fight—you will face challenges, and how you respond in those moments will define you. Prepare to stand up for yourself.

16. Forgive your enemies—especially yourself. Unshackle yourself from the prison of negative emotions like anger and blame, and create more space for hope and joy.

17. Have faith—set your course, and keep walking forward, trusting in yourself, and in the bigger picture.

And one more for the road …

18. Keep going—one action step every day will take you further than you can imagine.

Final reflection—Call to action

I would like to leave you with one last reflection in the form of a 'call to action'. In storytelling there is always a point early on where the hero is called to action to do something to solve the problem they have. Often the hero rejects the call to action at first, wary of leaving the familiar. Inevitably, the problem gets so pressing the hero is forced to take action, forced to step into an unknown world.

- Look at your story so far, what chapter do you find yourself in?
- What is working well in your story?
- What *bogus story* baggage do you need to dump, and replace with essential items, to continue on this journey?

You are the hero of your story.

- What do you want your life story to say?
- You write your map by making choices, so what choices do you need to make?
- The path unfolds as you take action, so what action do you need to take?
- What do you need to challenge yourself with?

The journey begins with you wanting to make a difference and you believing you can.

I call you to action

Remarkable You!

Final Travel Advisory

As I said at the beginning of this book, we all have a story, none more important than someone else's. Each story will be made up of many different chapters: some good, some bad and some downright ugly. But no matter our story, no matter our journey, or what stage of the journey we are on right now, I am sure we all want the same thing: we want our lives to matter.

I have shared a few chapters of my story in the hope of encouraging you to start this journey to discover hope, and to unshackle, reveal and enable the *remarkable* within *you*! I hope my story proves that although the gold within us is sadly often hidden, obscured by circumstances, every one of us has the option to believe in our worth and pursue our true potential. I know if you step forward boldly with courage, **Remarkable You** will be found! I believe in you. You matter!

We all get to determine how great our story is. We **all** get a blank page every day. We get to decide what that page will look like: we get to write on it. Will it be a living love letter that will influence others we meet on our journey?

Holocaust survivor Victor Frankl once said, "When we are no longer able to change a situation, we are challenged to change ourselves." As you have seen, it took intentional action to overcome the baggage of my history. I had to step up and take true responsibility for myself, my actions, my behavior, my growth and my future. You can too.

To grow you must be very willing to let your present and future be totally unlike your past. I want you to know, deep within every part of your being, *your history is not your destiny.* Do not keep settling for less than what you are meant to be.

Step into your potential.
Keep growing and keep going.
Keep that fire burning in your heart.

Journey well
Remarkable You!

"My grace is all you need; for my power is made strong in your weakness."
2 Corinthian's 12:9

Wendy Burns'

Essential Items for Remarkable Travelers

I do not know about you but I tend to over pack when I travel. To help you travel light, but with all the essential items, I have prepared a list of 10 essential items for you. It is time to dump the hidden baggage and fill up on what you need for the future—to make room, start by leaving the bogus stories behind!

1. **Self-Worth**—you are enough: right now, no matter what.
2. **HOPE**—Hang on in Patient Expectation that you always have a choice to step into your potential.
3. **FAITH**—find Future Answers In The Hope: trust in the bigger picture, even if you are not sure what it is.
4. **Energy**—be prepared play 'full out' on this journey of discovery.
5. **Strength**—everything worthwhile is uphill, but the outlook is worth the challenges of the climb.
6. **Courage**—it will not remove the obstacles, but it will show you how to forge a path that you believe in.
7. **Endurance**—you will never see the glory of the other side, the outcome you desire, unless you endure the uphill climb.
8. **Future Focus**—you must stop looking over your shoulder: you cannot walk forward while facing backwards.

9. **Forgiveness**—for those who have caused you harm, but especially for yourself.
10. **Curiosity**—stay open to possibility, and always be willing to learn and grow. The path will take you places you do not expect.

Journey well
Remarkable You

Download a free poster of this at www.remarkableyou.com.au

Epilogue: My Trust in God

Now let me acknowledge my Faith. My God.

Trust is such an interesting word. It means 'firm belief in the reliability or in the ability of someone or something'. It requires an action: an action of our hearts and mind. Right from my earliest childhood, my trust in other people was eroded by those who were meant to love, care for and protect me. Everything we do, all our confidence is drawn from our source of trust.

As children, we had no choice but to trust our parents, or those who raise us, will do anything to provide for us. We trusted their love and ability, and after that trust was eroded it took such a journey to learn how to trust again: ourselves, others and, for me, God.

My journey to discover the gold within me, required me to decide who God was for me. Would He be a vengeful God, one who would punish me—let me down like my earthly father had—or would I learn firsthand what the Bible means when it says:

> *"Those who put their trust in the Lord will renew their strength and soar on wings like eagles?"*
> **Isaiah 40:31**

You may think how this can be real? Why would God allow someone to experience all you have been through?

How can you worship a God you cannot trust? This is a question that hits at the heart of one of life's biggest decisions.

The biggest thing for me was simply this: would I be willing to trust this God is good, even when life is not? The answer for me was yes: maybe you feel the same way. Our response to pain and challenges determines so much about our future. In my desperation I reached out to God, and He was there, waiting for me.

Faith requires trust in something bigger than ourselves. By definition, we are placing trust in someone or something that is not always predictable, or even understandable, by human standards. Yet we humans want irrefutable proof of God's presence in our lives. God got my attention when that lady said, "God knows the guilt you have carried over you father's death. It was not your fault." Still, it took an epic journey from that moment to me completely understanding God was always going to be my choice: not something imposed by someone else, but *my choice*. That day in my lounge room, I reached my hand out in *faith* and there was a shift in my heart. God showed me I could trust Him even before I had relationship with Him.

After I decided to put my trust in God, I was no longer walking in my ability, but in the ability of God. The strength that came from God kept me moving forward in this journey of life. It also filled me with peace. Shame, stress, anxiety and guilt were replaced with God-given confidence in who I am. It has removed my fear, stepped me boldly into the call to be a *woman of influence*. It has healed my failures and filled me with grace. It wiped away my past and gave me a new hope and a great future.

I know life's storms, trials and pain will still come, but with Jesus in the storms with me, I may still be tossed around, but I will not sink nor be consumed by the storm.

> *"I believe if you keep your faith, you keep your trust, you keep the right attitude, if you're grateful, you'll see God open up new doors."*
> **Joel Osteen**

Lord, you know everything there is to know about me.
You perceive every movement of my heart and soul,
and you understand my every thought before it even enters my mind.
You are so intimately aware of me, Lord.
You read my heart like an open book
and you know all the words I'm about to speak
before I even start a sentence!
You know every step I will take before my journey even begins.
You've gone into my future to prepare the way,
and in kindness you follow behind me
to spare me from the harm of my past.
With your hand of love upon my life,
you impart a blessing to me
This is just too wonderful, deep, and incomprehensible!
Your understanding of me brings me wonder and strength.

Psalm 139: 1-6. The Passion Translation

"Keep your dreams alive. Understand to achieve anything requires faith and belief in yourself, vision, hard work, determination, and dedication. Remember all things are possible for those who believe."
Gail Devers

About the Author

Who is Wendy Burns?

Wendy Burns is a wife, mother and grandmother living in Queensland, Australia. From being born into impoverished circumstances, Wendy has become an international expert in professional coaching, transformational leadership, and is a practical business and personal coach, mentor, teacher and speaker.

In twenty years of leadership in various Australian government regulatory environments leading teams through organizational change, Wendy gained a reputation for consistently achieving efficiencies and innovation, alongside a track record of looking at the emotional health and well-being of staff, and addressing complex 'people situations' in multi-faceted, complex circumstances. To Wendy, people matter. After leaving the public sector, Wendy opened a consultancy business, working with individuals, diverse groups and teams in private corporations and the public sector. In 2013 Wendy joined the John Maxwell University (JMT), where (at the writing of this book) she serves as Peer Teaching Partner and Chair on the President's Advisory Council for JMT. By the invitation of the President of Paraguay in 2016, Wendy joined John Maxwell bringing transformational change to the nation.

Wendy has shared the stage with some of the most

influential leaders in the world, inspiring humanity to reach their potential by taking every opportunity to grow others and herself through her commitment to growth and action. She believes in lifelong learning.

Wendy believes every one of us is remarkable but we often cannot see it in ourselves. Wendy's passion is to empower people to become as remarkable as they were created to be; to reveal that vein of gold.

Wendy has helped many people experience extraordinary breakthroughs by enabling them to tap into their hidden gifts. She has a unique ability to press into, and challenge an individual's belief system, enabling them to unshackle, reveal and enable their most remarkable selves. She gets great joy from empowering others to open the door to a greater capacity by realizing their full potential.

To find out more about Wendy visit
www.wendyburnsconsulting.com.au

Do you wish Wendy could walk alongside you
on your remarkable journey?

Download your free copy of
Essential Items for Remarkable Travelers
or
subscribe to Wendy's email list
at

www.remarkableyou.com.au

and become part of her **remarkable** community today.

CPSIA information can be obtained
at www.ICGtesting.com
Printed in the USA
BVHW091954160922
647220BV00018B/710/J